College on a shoestring

A survival handbook for students

Eve Luddington

impact books

First published in Great Britain 1985
by **impact books**
112 Bolingbroke Grove, London SW11 1DA

Phototypeset by *Sunrise Setting,* Torquay, Devon.
Printed and bound in Great Britain by
Whitstable Litho Ltd., Whitstable, Kent.

British Library Cataloguing in Publication Data

Luddington, Eve
    College on a shoestring: a survival handbook
    for students.
    1. Home economics—Great Britain—Handbooks, manuals, etc.
    I. Title
    640'.941   TX57

    ISBN 0-245-54309-0

Contents

Preface

This book is exhaustive only in that it has exhausted me and my knowledge of student life. You'll discover your own ways of coping and enjoying yourself: I hope this will go some way towards helping you.

I'd like to thank my parents, without whom . . .! Also Audrey Coldron, Pat Murphy of Bretton Hall Students' Union and the following readers of *The Guardian* who answered my letter begging for tips:

Jim Barry, Ilford; Martyn Bennet, Loughborough; Dr. Marjorie Boulton, Oxford; Felicity Brayne, London W2; N. Joan Clark, Solihull; Maggie Coulthard, New Cross; J.H. Halliwell, Bolton; S. Hewitt, Dorchester; M.E. Howlett, Reading; Laura Keller, Bradford; Jacky Kitching, London NW3; Gillian Lake, Dyfed; Nora Lambe, Norwich; Vera Miller, Lincoln; John Ozimek, Bath; Mrs. Phil Plaskitt, Bedford; Ernie Roe, Ormskirk; Ruth, Wakefield (who was no help at all, but she did write a funny letter); Margaret Salter, Grantham; Alison Shaw, Huddersfield; Y. Taylor, Rainford; R.V. Wells M.A., Portsmouth.

I spent nearly seven years as a student after school, most of them in an idyllic place called Bretton Hall in Yorkshire. Too often I discovered, after the event, what I should have done: that's what prompted me to write this guide.

It's dedicated to David, who is either too shy or too worried that the book will be rubbishy, to want his surname published: his student days have just begun. I hope you enjoy yours.

1. Getting set for survival

Accommodation ■ your legal rights ■ pre-college preparation ■ grants ■ banks

Most freshers-to-be are inundated with college correspondence (and if you aren't, contact the registrar quickly because something is likely to be wrong!). Read everything carefully, even if it seems intimidating or boring, so that you may select from all the spiel to suit your own needs.

Two topics are probably top of your priority list at first: grants and accommodation. It is vital to get your grant claim in as early as possible – and that is more complicated than you might expect. If your parents are involved, they have to list earnings and outgoings, including mortgage situation, etc. Try to allow time for them to obtain all the necessary information and still send the claim in by June.

But once all the application forms are filed, there isn't much you can do about your grant unless or until the authority refuses it, so accommodation is likely to be your prime consideration.

Accommodation

It's amazing how much *where* you live affects *how* you live, so try to ensure you've a strong idea of what you might be letting yourself in for before you sign on any dotted lines. It would be ideal to visit the whole range of possible accommodation and talk to the present residents before making your own choice, but you might find that difficult, of course, if you live in John O' Groats and are about to study in Land's End. Instead, you could plod around local colleges/universities, checking out their living quarters: don't imagine that yours will be identical, but the trek should give you the "feel" of student accommodation generally (as well as sore feet).

The following outline might help your decision-making – skip it if you already understand the jargon of residence: it deals with basics!

Halls of residence

First refusal of halls of residence is often given to freshers. Halls (or hostels) are usually big boxes on or near campus containing single and/or double bedrooms for anything up to a hundred students. Bathroom and kitchen facilities are shared, but rarely between the entire resident population, as is the "common" room, if you're lucky enough to be provided with one.

A lot of comfort is laid on a plate for you in a hall: not only can you sleep later because you're close to college, you can also become acquainted with the area and its 'ambience' in the minimum time, because you're near college for 24 hours a day. Watch out, though, if the college is isolated from the "real world": there are times when you might feel you've had too much of a good thing.

You're provided with basic aids which are valuable if this is the first time away from home: all-in rent; simple cooking facilities and utensils; linen in some places – even cleaners occasionally! (Keep on the good side of cleaners; they treasure their favourites). For people who have never needed to budget before, the all-in rent prevents worrying about bills (you won't, yet, have to measure every drop of hot water or interrogate the one who left the fire on too long). However, remember that colleges do gain revenue from resident students – you'll have to accept that your rent will be relatively high, but do check before you move in that it isn't extortionate.

While you don't have to share bills with fellow students, you do have to share space, and you have no choice of whom you share it with. This need not be a terrific problem, if you're prepared. You're bound to meet new friends, but also – possibly – people with whom you have and want nothing in common. If you don't know by now the extent of your need for privacy, you'll soon discover it. And even if you're gregarious, the slight subject of *study* tends to hang over you, and often when others have free time. So you must suss out how you can find enough time to yourself without hibernating, and enough time for others without intruding.

It'll help to make your room – which might resemble a claustrophobic cell at first – comfortable for both work and relaxation. I used to set the desk first, away from any window to avoid "garden-gazing", and organise other gear around it. College rules vary when it comes to wall decoration, but most allow you to put up posters with blu-tack. If you're feeling ultra-efficient, find or make a cork pin-board for notes and messages. You could even put one in the corridor for general use.

As soon as you enter that corridor, "your" space is shared – so are the facilities in it – and so is noise. Actually, you needn't leave your room to share noise, so it's not wise to play stereos at full-blast late at night: the sleepless recipient of such blast will rarely complain aloud – it's more than a student's pride is worth – but resentment will fairly prickle, and that's not healthy for anyone.

So, hostel circumstances demand liberal doses of tolerance, for and from others. If you can keep on good terms with other residents, tolerance and thoughtfulness flow quite naturally, and life is a hell of a lot easier all-round. Sharing facilities *can* be mutually beneficial: if you've got two mugs and someone else has two spoonfuls of coffee, you're both made as long as no-one's nicked the kettle.

However, when it comes to your worldly goods, you should take a few precautions before you discover the need for them. First of all, insure all you own (see the end of *Accommodation* section for details), and then don't ruin your chance to claim for stolen goods by leaving your room unlocked. Additionally, label all valuables indelibly – on plastic and metal you can scratch your name with the point of a compass. The balance between over-caution and naive trusting is hard to attain, but it's worth finding. I'd advise against over-the-top deterrents such as burglar alarms or finger-traps for this reason; they tend to breed contempt and even temptation.

If you are to share storage space, get together with the others involved, and agree on a system of sharing; if it's not already decided for you by the allocation of lockers. In any case, label your food containers to avoid confusion, and remember to put your food in them: most midnight raiders only take food which is left out or anonymous, so that they can convince themselves it's theirs (don't mock; the "munchies" grab us all after a long night in the bar!). You're more likely to keep your provisions and good feeling if food is recognisably yours. By starting your term carefully but unfussily, you can avoid trouble; you should, anyway, be able to relax once you and your fellow inmates know each other.

It's uncanny how many times you'll hear words applied usually to prison, also bandied about college. In fact, college is nothing like prison (as far as I know), apart from the fact that both are institutions and tend to breed institutional grumbles.

One of the most common grouses concerns the canteen food. Fortunately for students, they are rarely in the prisoners' position of having to eat the food provided, or eating nothing: few colleges charge a bed-and-board rent to residents. If yours does, however, beware! You might lose out on the meals that you don't take: the meals you do take aren't necessarily edible, mainly because the cooks cater for hundreds of people with varying tastes and their "happy" medium tends to be bland, inoffensive and boring. Breakfast food might well be the exception to this generality, if my experience is anything to go by, perhaps because the numbers are down on other meals, perhaps because your taste buds aren't into excitement at that time in the morning.

So, if you can pay as you eat, do so – but then watch the prices – they're not cheap! Try to get the best nutritional value possible from such meals (see *Nutrition* in Chapter 4) and make the attempt to use that shared cooker in your hostel when you have time. You might feel trapped between the devil and the deep blue sea at first, but perhaps the best way of learning to cook is needing to eat.

The best way of learning to budget, however, is not by first being ripped off. Financial losing-out is a hazard for all colleges and one of their concerns at the moment, but you must ensure that the authority's cut-backs don't lead to the cutting out of all your comforts. Your college is unlikely to reduce your facilities, but it may not be able to replace worn ones – that's unfortunate but almost inevitable at the moment – and so the onus is on you to treat things carefully. If, though, the college attempts to raise your rent without obvious reason, question the decision, and get the backing of your Students' Union, too. The time to do this is when a rise is proposed, rather than when it's implemented, and also before your term's rent is in the authority's hands. You can't suddenly demand your money back when you see your bank balance and decide that you shouldn't have paid a higher rent ten weeks' earlier.

When you do want to move out of college you must, similarly, get in early. First speak to the person who deals with accommodation and arrange to leave at the end of a term, when you have used the place you've paid for. But if you wake up one day and think "I can't cope with this prison cell any longer!", don't panic immediately. Every student I've met has, at some time, felt trapped by college-life, especially if living on an isolated campus – it's the institutional blues. Expect this, and then you won't be caught out by the feeling into doing something daft. A good temporary cure for claustrophobia *à la* college is physical activity; anything from football to pool is therapeutic. It might also be a marvellous tonic to take one whole day away from the place with a friend who lives in the same hall. Only when frustration is ruining your life should you take steps to move out of college mid-term.

I seem to be offering a wealth of advice on what to do in awful circumstances: you might well be wondering why on earth anyone bothers to write such paragraphs of doom and despondency, or even why anyone ever goes to college. For one thing, if you expect the worst, you're always likely to be in for pleasant surprises; for another, it's useful to realise that college accommodation is no more perfect than any other. But take heart anyway – most people actually enjoy living in halls of residence!

Your hall will be your social centre as well as bed-sit when you start college. So, while responsibility is more difficult than usual to determine because so much is laid on that plate, if you enjoy your new home with an eye towards the comfort of others and their different demands, everyone should be fine.

For a suggested list of gear to take, see the end of this section, but do remember that the following are often forbidden in hostel rooms, and can produce more sparks than laughs if used with 5-amp "regulation" plugs (you may, of course, be able to use them in corridors): *electric fires/kettles/cooking equipment*.

College-approved accommodation

This includes, basically, any place which the college knows to exist and hasn't blacklisted. Possibly, the college will do all the admin work, leaving you to arrive at the shared flat, lodgings or bed-sit with nothing more to do than make yourself at home. More likely, you'll find the address from college and do the rest of the work yourself. Similarly various is the amount of protection offered by college. Generally, the more admin the college undertakes, the more responsibility they accept for your "pad". A big advantage of college-approved accommodation of any type is that, in most cases, other students have coped with it before you. Also, the rent is likely to be compatible with your grant. If there is a resident landlord or lady, he or she is probably sympathetic to students; and if the worse happens and the place is uninhabitable in any way, you may save others from your fate by informing college. If your college is situated in a city or where rents are generally high, you're lucky to be offered this relatively cheap accommodation; anyway, most places of your own are preferable to most mattresses on friends' floors.

Some of these college-approved places offer bed and breakfast, with the breakfast included in the rent. It might be an idea when you find yourself in one of these, to force down a massive breakfast and forget the snack lunch from a canteen – which might be pricey – or make sandwiches to take with you to college. Be wary, though, of rents which include an evening feed. Before your course begins, you might well intend to be in by mealtime every night: the demands of either the course or your social life could wreck that resolution, while the rent remains the same. And where the evening meal is not included, make sure that you can obtain one which is cheap and nutritious: check the facilities you're offered – access to one gas ring is heaven compared with the hay box you may otherwise have to use (if you *do* need a hay box – which is *very* cheap to run, see Chapter 4, *What to eat* section).

Check also the "rules of the house". Although most student landlords/ladies are quite enlightened, you may come across one who, for instance, forbids members of the "other" sex to cross the threshold: decide before you take the lodging whether such rules suit you (gays – for once you might benefit from discrimination!). If they don't and you've got to take the place, you can either ignore the rules quietly and hope for the best, or make yourself so affable that the rules are dropped. The best way to avoid problems is to visit the accommodation before your need is desperate, so that you can look at the place objectively and in a relaxed state of mind: if you do come across problems, you might have to decide on that friend's mattress for a while, after all.

The following types of accommodation may come under the broad heading of "college-approved", or they may be discovered through estate agents or on the grapevine. I reckon they're worth noting separately because each type has delights and drawbacks of its own.

Bed-sits

Bed-sits can, again, be havens or holes. If you move into one as a fresher, the chances are that you've found it for yourself. Remember that any meals which are provided for you are an extension of "home": they save the bother of cooking, but may demand a commitment which you can't or won't make. Such bed-sits tend to be rooms in the house of a family, and a hell of a lot of happiness depends upon how well you get on with that family. I once had a place in central London which worked out fantastically; I paid virtually no rent in return for occasional dusting, very rare babysitting (for a boy who was too old to scream all night) and frequent, interesting chats with the lonely lady of the house. If ever I wanted a meal, I was included with the others without constant obligation; I even felt at home enough to cook for them sometimes and we all mucked in together happily. Such luck is rare – as I've since discovered – but it's not impossible by any means, particularly if there's give and take around.

If you're "self-contained", your room is largely what you make it. You can choose your own company and your privacy, so your comfort and your socialising depend on you. Don't be too shy to borrow "a cup of sugar" or to lend one – many a friendship begins with a cliché. You can, in such a way, meet people outside the college set-up, relatively easily; this might appeal, particularly, to "seasoned" or mature students. If you're a "fresh" fresher who's into discovering college life, this type of accommodation may not suit you so well: it involves more independence, more responsibility and more effort than others. But there's one big advantage for anyone who either doesn't have to make an effort to make friends or enjoys being a "loner": in a bed-sit, the lack of imposed distractions can lead to conscientious study!

Shared accommodation

Shared accommodation (sometimes furnished, sometimes not) with people of your own choice is often the chosen domain of second and third year students; it's less likely that freshers will move straight away into such places. Even so, it's worth understanding their set-up.

If you're compatible and happily organised, shared houses or flats are often the cheapest accommodation and the most fun. When it comes to eating, they are certainly the most interesting if everyone mucks in with the cooking: where cooking is taken in turn, variety is welcome; where each person contributes something to each delight, I hope you enjoy living dangerously. Chapters 2 and 3 deal more fully with the ins-and-outs of sharing facilities in these circumstances, so for now I'll offer more basics as to the actual living situation.

Sharing accommodation usually means sharing friends and ideas without killing yourself to make an almighty effort: even if you're sharing with the "wrong" people, a social circle of sorts tends to evolve. In any college accommodation, you'll probably learn to tolerate more than you ever thought possible: if that doesn't come easily you'll need to cultivate it, particularly in shared accommodation, because there it is vital!

You're expected to do your share of the housework in such

places. So it's important to know the rudiments of washing up for a
household; of washing and ironing for yourself, and of leaving
bathrooms and kitchens as you find them (or better). If you do none
of these jobs you can still "get by" – especially if you're loaded with
charm – but you won't half be resented. Discover these basics from
"mum" (okay, any housekeeper, but mum's the one who usually is
lumbered) during the summer, if you've never thought about them
before. Also learn how to mend clothes and how to deal safely with
electricity so that it doesn't give you more than you expected in the
way of a buzz.

Most important, and a tip for all students: try not to assume if
you're male that washing, mending etc., should be passed to the
handiest female or, if you're female, that any fuse you attempt to
change is going to blow the house up. The basic message is "don't
use or be used by people", which is a completely different kettle of
fish from lending, borrowing and sharing: usurpers learn nothing
of value, and the used discover more bitterness than they knew they
had; those who share sensibly are often the happiest.

Overall – particularly north of the Watford Gap where rents are
generally quite low – shared accommodation is the cheapest you're
likely to find; for rent, for food-sharing and for readily available
social life. Frustrating, infuriating it may be sometimes; fulfilling
and fun it almost certainly will be!

Living "at home"

Living "at home" on the other hand, might be the one type of
accommodation in which you scarcely notice the difference
between your past and present life. If you live close to college, you
may have no choice but to stay with your parents or guardians. In
that case, try not to treat the college as a nine-to-five "job", nor to
treat your home as a hotel, but find a balance between the two. Most
students enjoy the peculiarities of student life, and not only if they're
free from family ties for the first time. Suddenly, you have the
chance to meet people from entirely different backgrounds, with
diverse experiences, views and ideals. It's easy to hide from the
unfamiliar if you have the constant security of "home" enveloping

you, but you'll be missing out on a heck of a lot of your education – you're at college for far more than obtaining a qualification in a specific subject. As a student, you have the chance to discover a broad spectrum of life; enjoy it to the full!

Off-beat accommodation

Of course, there are unmentioned (and some unmentionable) forms of accommodation. Some of the places I've mentioned will be unfurnished, though most freshers would be advised not to move into them straight away. If you do own some furniture, the unfurnished places are cheap to rent, but what you save is hardly enough to pay for all the other furniture that you'll find you want, even if you spend all your waking hours hunting markets and second-hand shops for bargains.

Unusual accommodation includes sleeping in college baths (generally a temporary measure after a late night, and only recommended where porters are either very friendly or blind); sleeping on friends' floors or – in the case of someone I know – sleeping in a car for a term to save rent money. A bit of roughing it won't hurt anyone, but desperate measures should be reserved, I reckon, for desperate needs – and are not suitable for freshers. Seriously, though, you might have problems finding somewhere habitable if you're living in London or other big cities: there's a London section later in the guide, which might be of some use.

You shouldn't underestimate your need for some sort of "base", especially when you begin college. On the other hand, try to learn as much as you can about this new life as soon as you can: the sooner the preliminaries are over, the more easy it is to settle in.

Your legal rights

Although it's the unlucky student who needs to assert them, it's useful to know your rights concerning accommodation, especially if you're a private tenant. There are quite a lot of tenants' rights, actually, but it might take you ages of wading through red tape to actively obtain them.

Estate agents

Apart from the grapevine, estate agents can be helpful in finding
you accommodation. They're not allowed to charge you a penny
for simply putting you on a list, or even for giving you a list of
landlords' addresses. If they ask for money, and you need a place,
pay what they want and get into your accommodation *before* you
claim a fee back. If they do more work for you, and actually find you
a place to live, they are entitled to charge.

Landlords and landladies

When you've finally found accommodation, you shouldn't be
charged a premium or "key money" in most unfurnished places,
nor in furnished ones where the rent is registered by a rent tribunal.
If the landlord/lady does, make sure you receive a receipt; take that
and your complaint to the local Citizens' Advice Bureau. You can
legally be charged a deposit – which is different – but it should be
returned when you move out (unless, I suppose, you've not paid
your rent for umpteen weeks, or have wrecked the joint).

For your part as a tenant, you're entitled to a rent book which
states the landlord's name and address; his/her agent (if any); the
rent; rates, and details of the local rebate scheme. This rent book, by
the way, is a vital possession when you claim supplementary benefit
from the DHSS during the summer holidays. I'd say it's always
better to keep on friendly terms with your landlord but if a rent
book is refused – even after you've used all your powers of charm
and persuasion – complain to your local council.

Be prepared if a cunning landlord tries to raise your rent. Before
blowing your top, check the rents of comparable properties in your
area, so long as they're not owned by the same person! If you think
you're going to be ripped off – or even if you're being overcharged
with your present rent – you can appeal to the Rent Tribunal.
Officially, a landlord can't, anyway, raise rent without asking the
Rent Tribunal and, if the property is registered, it's unlikely that
anything can be done until three years after registration date.

It's important, though, to check other rents before you appeal
about yours: a Rent Officer can increase as well as decrease what you

must pay. If you disagree with what he demands, you have the fall-back of appealing to your local Rent Assessment Centre, but such extra hassle takes time and stamina.

It takes time, too, for the landlord to repair the accommodation. He/she is responsible for repairing the structure, the exterior, plumbing and gas fittings. If you're waiting for ages for essential work to be done, and the fault is dangerous or damaging to your health, you can speed things up a lot by threatening to go to the Public Health Department, which deals with complaints. You, too, must keep your side of the bargain. Any agreement you've made to "keep in good repair" mustn't be ignored: in fact, everyone will be happier in the long run if you keep your accommodation in reasonable order.

If you're suddenly told to quit, take note of how it's done: it's got to be in writing, and the notice must expire on a rent day. The only way you can actually be forced to leave is by court order, which will give you at least four weeks' notice.

The local Citizens' Advice Bureau is the place to contact if you have any problems about accommodation which you can't sort out for yourself, and as the housing laws are so complicated, it might be best to rush down there as soon as any accommodation difficulties occur.

Benefits

Anyone (except overseas students who might be penalised for daring to ask for aid) who lives in a hall of residence or other rented place, loses nothing by applying for *housing benefit*. You apply to the local council and the benefit is assessed according to your income – students are often in with a chance of help – and the NUS recommends that students give it a try.

As with every application, make sure yours is well-worded and easy to read: legibility puts assessors in a better frame of mind!

Pre-college preparation

Having waded through accommodation lists and stuck a pin in your preference, there are other preparations to be made before college starts. Whatever the type of place you're going to live in try to find out, before you get there, what you need to take in the way of equipment.

Equipment
You won't necessarily begin term with all the gear but here's a list of things which you're most likely to need or want from the word 'go'.

Definites:
- clothes and clothes hangers
- shoe cleaning kit
- laundry bag and washing powder
     (maybe just a plastic sack)
- books
- stamps and envelopes
- paper (letter and working)
- pens, pencils, rulers, glue etc.
- toiletries
- scissors
- aspirin etc.
- food containers
- sticky labels
- knife
- mugs
- coffee, tea etc.
- alarm clock

Possibilities
(some of these will be needed only if you're a non-resident student):
- duvet
- bed linen

- towels
- spare plugs and fuses
- screwdriver and other basic tools
- radio, cassette/record player etc.
- basic cooking utensils
- box of preservable foods
- typewriter
- TV (?!)

It might help you to circulate this list among family and friends, in case anything that they were about to chuck out could be put instead to your good use. If, by any chance, you're stuck without basics, try army surplus stores for bed linen and towels, or markets for other gear.

As I've said before (and, no doubt, will repeat again), do insure all these worldly goods.

Insurance

There are two companies which cater specifically for students, and very few others which will give you a look-in, because students are "bad risks". From both *Endsleigh Insurance Services Ltd* (97, Southampton Row, London WC 1 – Tel: 01 580 4311) and *Harrison Beaumont Ltd* (69, High Street, Witney, Oxford – Tel: 0993 3251) you can obtain insurance, whatever your accommodation, for goods and travel. Endsleigh is the only insurance company recognised by the NUS, but Harrison Beaumont was the first in the student market: with either, you've a good chance of being treated sympathetically. Even if you think you're taking very little with you to college at first, do use the insurance available – little is a lot more than nothing.

So far, I've only dealt with what you're likely to need (or want) if you're living in college, and already there's quite a bit of money involved. If you live out of college, there's a lot more to come! Where you're provided with a room and use of a kitchen, you're going to need stuff to cook with.

Kitchen equipment

For basic kitchen equipment, stroll around markets and jumble sales. You don't really need much but, if you're self-catering, you'll do much better by having the *right* stuff:

- *Knife*: A strong, sharp knife is more important than forks and spoons – you can always use fingers to eat, but it's messy to rip up raw meat or cheese. Good knives are pricey at the outset, but can be sharpened and are almost everlasting (*Don't* leave any wooden-handled ones in water).

- *Chopping board*: This is vital if you don't want to upset your landlord. If you can, find a hardware shop to sell you an off-cut. Tell the assistant what it's to be used for – splintered wood is good for the teeth but adds a peculiar texture to your cooking. Use one side of the board for onions and similar smellies, and the other for food not to be contaminated by strong smells.

- *Decent pan*: One pan is the absolute minimum. A general (and generalised, no doubt) rule with pans is the heavier, the better. Actual "non-stick" pans need to be treated very carefully; it might be wiser to find one without that dubious "attraction" but still of the best quality you can afford.

- *Wooden spoon*: Very useful for many jobs (again, don't leave it in water).

- *Fish slice*: A wide spatula with long, narrow slits, this tool is used to get things out of shallow pans. If you do have a coated pan of any sort, use a plastic fish slice. Don't leave it over heat.

- *Tin opener*: Preferably one with a corkscrew and bottle opener as well.

- *Cutlery*: If you're *very* poor and into primitive living, your good knife and wooden spoon will suffice – I recently discovered that Medievals managed perfectly with nothing else in the way of cutlery – I suppose you could always chop up your spaghetti. However, most street markets sell the more sophisticated equipment quite cheaply: a couple of forks, teaspoons, dessertspoons and tablespoons are useful; the spoons can be used for measuring amounts of food as well as for eating it.

■ *Crockery*: Get as many mugs as you can muster; they can be used to store left-overs as well as for drinking. At least one bowl and a few plates will be useful, too.

■ *Glasses*: Glasses aren't essential really, but they seem to add taste to that occasional(?) beer.

■ *Containers* Plastic containers for food are free, if you can scrounge from someone who buys ice cream or marge in quantity. Without their lids, they can be used to store fruit and veg as well as the usuals.

Some sweetshops still use huge glass jars which they'll sell you cheaply (or even give you). It's probably better to wait until you've arrived at college before hunting them down, but they are useful and decorative as flour, pasta and sugar containers. Having them also allows you to buy such stuff in quite large quantities, which will be relatively cheap.

Used coffee jars can be used for similar purposes, while mustard containers and the like – as well as pill-jars from chemists – make good herb containers.

Biscuit tins are efficient when you want to store – biscuits! Make sure you don't put soft and crunchy ones in the same tin, or you'll have wasted the crunch.

I think I've listed above the absolute essentials but there are, of course, many more utensils which will be useful, including:

■ *Frying pan*: A big, deep one is probably the best, basically because it's flexible in use. Again, don't worry too much about the "non-stickers", as long as you can find one which isn't going to rust as soon as it sees water.

■ *Small saucepan*: You've far more choice of when and what to cook if you've an extra pan, and a small one uses less fuel. If you're clever, you can even put it on top of a bigger pan and use only one ring.

■ *Mixing bowl*: This is valuable for an infinite variety of occasions. If you're likely to heat food in it over a saucepan (fuel-saving, once more), don't buy a plastic one – although plastic is cheaper to buy and useful for most purposes. Pyrex or pottery bowls are pricey, but heatproof. Lidded ones are, of course, more useful still.

- *Egg-whisk*: Not vital but it is less tiring on your wrists than a fork or spoon, and it can be used with many foods other than eggs.
- *Sieve*: Apart from saving lumpy sauces from the bin, it has many uses.

If you have rich or generous relatives, there are several "electricals" which are very helpful to students, especially to those who can't afford the time to spend hours preparing cheap meals.

- *Electric kettle*: As well as being quicker than an ordinary kettle or pan of water, the electric kettle saves space on the cooker, and money on the fuel bill if used properly. Where you otherwise need to use an immersion heater to warm water, it's cheaper to heat it in a kettle when you need to use only a little.
- *Slow-cooker*: Akin to a hay-box (see Chapter 4, *What to eat* section), but rather more sophisticated, a slow-cooker is a miracle object which cooks during the day if you chuck the grub in before you leave home in the morning. Stews and casseroles are cooked very cheaply and painlessly in a slow-cooker, much more cheaply than in an oven – it uses the same amount of fuel as a light bulb!
- *Dry fryer*: This is very useful if you want your fried food without the fat; you need to get used to the lack of greasiness, but it's worth it for the slim, spot-free and healthy-hearted person it helps you to be.
- *Electric frying pan*: Not quite as healthy as the above, it's nevertheless sworn by some to be the only thing you need for cooking: it is very versatile, but . . .!
- *Liquidiser*: Lovers of soup and other mushy food derive great pleasure from watching a liquidiser do the job of a sieve, effortlessly, more efficiently and in moments.
- *Micro-wave*: Okay, okay: this *is* a wildly optimistic recommendation. It's surprising how many students do, in fact, have access to such luxuries, but I'm not daring to suggest that you blackmail anyone into buying you one. However, if you can

use one, it's cheap because it cooks so quickly. A friend and I worked out that if you lashed out on a micro-wave with your first term's grant, and lived on nothing but baked potatoes (which take just minutes to do in some of them) and cheese, you'd made your money back by the end of the year (of course, our arithmetic needs checking!).

The big advantage of the micro-wave is its almost incredible speediness, and its consequent saving of fuel.

The big disadvantage, which also applies to most "extras", is that it's pricey to buy in the first place. For some it might also take the fun out of what can – surprise, surprise – be the enjoyable pastime of cooking.

■ *Pressure cooker*: In some ways, this is a poor man's (woman's) micro-wave. Of course, it's not quite so speedy, nor quite so versatile, but it does cook food very quickly, while retaining all the vitamins and minerals possible. It's also extremely useful if you have only one or two gas/electric rings, because it can come with three separate compartments per pan.

Overall I'd say that the more cooking utensils you can beg, borrow or . . . , the more likely it is that you'll enjoy cooking and experimenting with food: these utensils, together with a few cookery books, are adult toys!

Study materials
From food for the body to food for the mind – well, I thought there was a natural link! If you value your friends, don't leave valuable pens and suchlike lying around, only to discover that they disappear. Stealing is an inevitable evil of most colleges and careless borrowing occurs everywhere. Anyway, everyone loses pens when they use them frequently, at odd times and in various places; so, while you might well be cursing a "friend", your treasured pen could have been lost innocently. In any case, you want to avoid bad feeling whatever the cause: I'd suggest buying packs of tatty biros for the most part, rather than one "special" writing implement.

When it comes to paper, of which most students use a lot, find a

cheap stationer, or a friend from whom you can obtain good stocks.
Many large colleges have cheap stores of their own, but if you're
moving from town to country you might find that the college shop
is a relative rip-off. However, don't bother to take enough stocks
for three terms – chances are that you'll return to your cheap shop
before the end of the term and, anyway, paper is heavier to transport
in bulk than you'd expect. In addition, a small stock of envelopes,
notebooks, personal files, sticky tape, scissors, blu-tack etc., is
useful to have before you get to college (as well as a stash of coins to
phone your relatives when you realise what "vitals" you've
forgotten).

You're going to have to decide before you travel to college, what
your priorities are concerning the amount you first take with you. If
you've plenty of facilities for transporting, it's wise to remember
that you might – in the leisure of your summer holiday – look more
closely for bargains than you ever will during term-time. On the
other hand, there are very strong student concessions in some areas
– and particularly if you're studying Art – which might make
buying at college (and therefore carrying from home) lighter work.

Set books

Beware the college booklist! Don't buy every book diligently
before terms starts – the list may be published to impress other
people than students (the DES for example). If you're raring to
study, borrow books from your local library over the summer
(order them if they're not on the shelves): it's only when you arrive
at college that you discover precisely which books *need* to be
bought. Such books are the ones you'll be using regularly – source
books on the whole. Others can be borrowed from the college
library – if you get there soon enough – or borrowed from friends:
there are even some student unions who have a very cheap budget
sale of "set" books discarded by past (or present!) students.
Photocopying is a dodgy subject: you're advised not to do it until
you've discovered copyright rules from the person in charge of the
machine.

Often there are on your booklist publications by your very own lecturers: that sounds good at first (someone you know is famous – and stuff like that), but do be careful to take these books on their own merit rather than on the advice of the booklist. By all means read them, but don't buy them until you know how relevant they are to you. One person who wrote to me suggested one very good reason for reading your lecturers' books – and that was to be able to quote from them when appropriate. He added that – God forbid! – you'll give yourself a chance of better grades if you know them verbatim. I'll add that although, obviously, the lecturers want you to buy their books to line their pockets, it's also true that they're unlikely to have written them solely to make money; their philosophy (and perhaps that of their department) is probably lurking in those books, and that philosophy concerns you when you're on their course.

Books generally, seem to be a great attraction for students whether you read them or not. "Cheap" secondhand books might be useful – but they may not be. Buying a job-lot for one item you fancy is certainly not advisable. So try not to indulge in this habit until you're aware of how much money is taken up by other articles which might be more important – and until you're sure that you'll have the time and inclination to read more than the front covers of any "bargains". In fact, it's better not to launch on any pricey hobby until your budget is flowing nicely.

Travel
Strictly speaking, travel shouldn't be included in pre-college preparation, I suppose, but it is something worth thinking about before you begin college.

In theory, your grant bears the cost of three return journeys "home" yearly. Obviously, you're unlikely to be able to make the first trip to college cheaply if you have to rely on public transport, what with hauling heavy luggage around; after that you might well be able to economise on the standard cost.

See whether it's worth investing in a *Railcard*, obtainable from British Rail stations, or in a *Coachcard* (from National Express coach stations). Either entitles you to half-price tickets – or thereabouts –

at most times. You'll need your NUS card before buying the Coachcard, but not for the Railcard if you're under 24 years old.

Bikes, of course, are the cheapest form of transport after Shanks's pony, but are also one of the most nickable. If you take one to college first insure it, then buy a heavy padlock which is resistant to evil articles like hacksaw blades. An extra deterrent for prying hands, and an aid to recovery if the bike is pinched is coding; so although very few stolen bikes are seen again by their owners, it's worth asking your local Crime Prevention Officer to code it. This involves making an appointment at your local police station where the job is done for free.

When you park, make sure your bike is in an open, busy place, and take with you any detachables like lamps and pumps.

The same basic rules apply to motorbikes except that if you want yours coded, you'll have to do it yourself – with a compass point or something similar.

Four wheels are, for most students, too expensive to run; if you do own a car, you'll agree! However, cars are very convenient – particularly if your college is out in the wilds – and can even be economical if you are generous with lift-giving. Try to help and be helped by transporting friends around, and splitting the petrol costs. Don't be scared to ask for payment; you're providing a very useful service which might be cheaper and is certainly more cosy than public transport – and if you give fair warning of your price, objectors can do the other thing!

With all your deals and dealings, remember that every student is, or should be, on the same low income as you; any tips you discover before or at college to save money and hassle, deserve to be passed on and shared. However, there is one thing you cannot share with anyone else: your individual ways and means of getting your own full grant entitlement.

Grants

Nowadays, very few students depend for their grant purely upon the local authority, so it's vital that parents or other sponsors, realise how important their contribution is.

If you're dependent upon your parents, and they're willing to pay what they should, you might be nicely surprised by a fairly new scheme: the *parental deed of covenant*.

Covenants

Assuming you're over 18 years old (or married if under 18) and your parents pay tax, they can formally agree to pay you a certain amount of money (presumably their specified contribution) regularly for more than six years. Don't let that "six years" rule bug you or them, it's not binding: if you're careful with the wording, the agreement can be abandoned or altered after your student days. But, as long as you don't earn enough during your vacations to be taxed, there's tax relief while it is paid. Therefore, your parents may deduct a third of the specified grant contribution from what they pay out, while you claim the extra because you're not eligible for tax: just fill in form IR185AP from the local tax office, at the end of March (which is the end of the financial year). The only problem with this is that you might need the money at other times: if so, your parent may give you the full amount owing, and you return the amount that comes back in tax relief when it arrives.

Your parents' contribution is likely to vary from year to year, depending on their circumstances and the government's award policies: because of that you might find it easiest to draw up a *variable amount covenant*. There's a specimen of one below: replace the words in italics with your own, and make sure the deed is dated before the first payment is due. Also make sure that there's no money to be paid during holidays or problems might set in. The completed document should be signed by a witness, and sealed to make it official. Keep two copies, one for you and one for your parents. Finally, remind your parents to keep a record of all their incomings and outgoings – they'll need it for tax claims.

I, *A.N. Other* of *1, Thingummy Street, Thingummy, Thingummyset,* covenant to pay my *daughter Dodie* of *the same address,* the gross amount as specified below on each of the following dates in each year, *namely 1 October, 1 January* and *1 April,* for the period of seven years, or for the period of our joint lives, or until *she* ceases to be receiving full-time education at any university, college, school or other educational establishment (whichever is the shortest period), the first payment to be made on *1 October 1986.*

The gross amount of each such payment shall be one-third of the parental contribution towards *Dodie Other's* student maintenance grant for the year in which the payment is made, calculated according to any regulations for the time being in force relating to mandatory awards by local education authorities.

Dated *15 September 1986*
Signed, sealed and delivered by *A.N. Other*

(signature) .... SEAL ....
in the presence of
   Ann Ominous, 2, Blank Buildings,
   Thingummy, Thingummyset.

You may otherwise have a *fixed amount covenant,* but if you use that, the old one must be cancelled (or a new one added) when the grant contribution is changed by the authority. The advantage of the fixed covenant is that a ready-printed copy can be obtained from your local tax office (covenant form IR47).

If you're still confused, more detailed info is published in the September 1983 issue of *Which?* magazine, which should still be available from The Consumers' Association, 14, Buckingham Street, London WC2N 6DS.

I'm possibly making the whole idea seem a hell of a lot of both but who could refuse a bit of faffing when you get this wonderful "cut-price" offer?

Unwilling contributors

If you are one of the many whose parents can't or won't pay their official contribution, you've got problems. It's hoped they'll raise any objections when their pay demand comes from the authority, so that you have fair warning, and can act in good time. While there are painful answers to this problem, it'll probably help everyone more if you "play it cool" at first: they might have fair reasons for their refusal. Have your parents' circumstances changed since the assessment was made? If, for example, one or both parents have been made redundant or retired, they can appeal and are generally treated sympathetically. If your parents can but would rather not pay their contribution, you must make it clear to them (in the nicest possible way!) that your grant is not pocket money, but is actually living expenses. You might make up a sensible budget of what you expect to spend and on what, or use an actual budget worked out by a present student. Finally, you might remind your parents that they're legally bound to pay their contribution and, to avoid this responsibility, they must disown you!

In fact, there's little more you can do to obtain your full grant unless you take your parents to court – and this would probably cause them to disown you, if they hadn't before! Whilst no other method is guaranteed, the NUS at your college might help you to apply pressure – they're bound to have had experience of this problem. The main bind is that this action would be taken after your authority grant has arrived, and might take too long to be of any immediate use.

Arrival (or non-arrival) of grants

At the beginning of any term, but especially your first, there are unusual costs: therefore, it's worthwhile having some cash with you in case your grant doesn't arrive promptly. Avoid starting an overdraft with the bank before you've deposited a penny – it doesn't endear you to the manager – even if your grant is very late.

Late grants occur for several reasons: if you put in your claim very late, you're more likely to have hassles; if your local education authority has more applicants than staff to deal with them, they have hassles. But after a week or two of delay, for whatever reason, ask a college official to phone your local education offices; he/she will carry more weight than you.

Banks

By the time your grant arrives, you'll already be aware that banks
are eager to acquire student customers. Whilst they earn peanuts
from you as a student, their attracting you now might pay dividends
"when" you're a rich graduate.

Before you plump for the one with the prettiest cheques, or
fanciest offers, it might be an idea to sit down and consider your
own finances; suss out how much (or how little) there is to play
with. You could work out a proposed termly budget, taking
everything into account – right down to the amount you intend to
spend on your third cousin at Christmas. While you're doing this,
remember that you receive about 35% of your grant in the Autumn
and Spring terms (to see you through the holidays), but only 30%
during the Summer term – Supplementary Benefit is supposed to be
your "wage" during the summer holiday, unless you get a job.

Apart from scaring you silly, this activity is a startling revelation:
there's no way you're rich on your grant; there's no way you're
going to get a huge amount of interest on your "capital" – in fact,
there's no way, yet, that you can use the bank except as a coffer and
lender (anyone who knows different, please contact my publisher!).
But however enormous your fright when you do a few sums, the
thing is to remain cool: ironically, the student's dread of poverty can
be the cause of the worst problems. This statement might well seem
daft, but take for example, the overdraft agreement: that means
you're withdrawing money you don't possess. In spite of all the
"logical" worry involved, the actual process has a curious buzz to it:
it even makes you feel wealthy – you feel as if you've been given a
present. Of course you know in the back of your mind that you're
going to repay the loan eventually, and with interest.
Unfortunately, in this commercial society, it's very easy for that
realisation to remain firmly plonked in the *back* of your head. The
moral of this paragraph: don't overdraw unless it's to finance a very
lucrative project.

Morals are one thing, of course; practicalities are a vastly different
matter for many: in fact, it is estimated that about one-fifth of all

students are more than £100 overdrawn at the beginning of the summer; many have an overdraft by mid-term. So, while you are frugal, it's probably best to still accept the possibility of overspending and to vow to stay sane if/when this situation occurs.

For a start, when you're choosing a bank, forget the "exciting" frills offered by some banks to attract you – articles such as cheap Railcards, book tokens and subscriptions to well-known periodicals etc. Instead, first investigate the basic facilities offered.

Overdrafts

At the time I'm writing, three of the four big banks have special overdraft facilities for students: they don't lend money "gratis", but they do charge less interest than usual for students who borrow. A bank which offers such fundamentals plus frills, might be a good bet, but do get your priorities sorted out first.

If/when you do need an overdraft, it's up to you to write to your bank manager, asking, "Please may I . . .?' (This is where the importance of recording exactly what you spend shows). Letters from the bank, beginning, "According to our accounts . . . ' and ending, "phone to make an appointment", bode ill for future arrangements. If you do have to meet the manager at any time, he's likely to be more genial if you have some idea of your finances.

Plastic money

In spite of the problems many students encounter with money, nothing will stop the banks offering you "easy" means of spending when you open your account: there are cheque cards, hole-in-the-wall (cashpoint) cards and even credit cards (Access/Visa). Unless you're very careful with your records, these plastic monies can lead to great difficulties, since they make it very easy to forget how much you've spent.

In theory, there are huge advantages to be had from cheque cards. In conjunction with a cheque, they can be used at most shops; they also allow you to withdraw up to £50 at any branch of your bank free, and for a small payment you can withdraw that amount from any bank. Any cheque you issue that has your cheque card number on the back is guaranteed for an amount up to £50. When I was a student, this facility seemed fantastic – until I started using my cheques to buy the next packet of tea bags. Then I returned the card! Without it, you are still able to withdraw from more than one branch, if you have a cashpoint card.

Cashpoint cards give you free use of the automatic cash dispensers owned by your bank. I'd advise you to make an arrangement with your branch, so that money is refused if you're overdrawn (if it is not already the case); otherwise, you can amass quite a debt this way, too. Assuming you have a cashpoint within easy reach, the machine prevents the hassles of writing cheques and queueing for the cashier. The various banks have different ruling on the amounts you can withdraw and when, so check this out.

When it comes to Access/Visa, try not to be tempted; you're not really in the wage-bracket to benefit from them, and keeping the waiting *in* the wanting is good for character-building anyway!!

Which branch?
Since you'll be spending more time at college than in your parental home, it's better to pick a branch near to where you study. Unless you're with Girobank, which is based in post offices and opens during post office hours, make sure that you'll be able to reach your branch during banking hours. After that, assuming you're in the ideal situation of still having a wide choice, suss out which bank gives you the most favourable long-term deal. Actually, nothing prevents you from opening more than one account if you think that might work best.

I'd advise definitely, however, against joining your parents' branch: the bank might be rather too eager to use them as "guarantors", which is bad for your independence, and might become bad for parent/child relationships.

Whichever, or however many, banks you choose, remember always that the bank is there to serve you – after all, you will be paying for the service one day! Don't be frightened of the manager or, if that suggestion's beyond all hope, don't let on that you're scared. In any dealings, try to give the impression that you can cope successfully with your finances under "normal" circumstances.

At the risk of boring you with repetition, I'll suggest again that it's very helpful to write all your money dealings in your cheque book. Know how much you have in your account and act accordingly: try not to fall into the "extravagance" trap when you're overdrawn – the "might as well be hanged for a sheep" attitude can have terrible consequences.

If the worst comes to the worst, and there's not a penny in that account, nor have you a cheque card (because they've whipped it off you), you'll have to swallow your pride and have a good talk with the bank manager. "Rubber" cheques – those which bounce – aren't a solution to any problem, as you'll know if you've ever felt the bitterness attached to receiving one.

Bank accounts are necessary; and if you play the bank's game without falling for its tricks to extort "extras" from you, you needn't go far wrong. I suppose the only way of avoiding the risk of banking hassles – the only sure way – is to open an account and withdraw all the money as soon as your grant cheque is cleared. The advantage of this is that you'll always be spending cash and, somehow, you know better how much you're spending when it's in coins and notes. The obvious disadvantage, apart from losing it at one go, is the landlord's wrath when he/she discovers the mattress you've slashed to store your notes!

2. Freshers' week and beyond

Freshers' week ■ after freshers' week ■ loneliness ■ drugs ■ coping with study ■ sex ■ the law ■ help and advice ■ making a bit on the side ■ holidays

Freshers' Week

By the time I was a "seasoned" student, I used to look forward all through summer to Freshers' Week. This was when we "oldies" felt very important – showing the ropes to new students; getting very drunk on our newly-arrived grants, and enjoying the events supposedly set up for freshers – "What freshers?!!" Such highs will be yours too, but not in the first year unless you're amazingly adaptable: Freshers' Week isn't really there for freshers, I reckon.

Instead, in your very first few days at college, you're likely to find this pattern in essence, if not specifics. This is how I remember it.

Societies' Fair

Follow the mob into a hall – *another* hall. There are hundreds of weirdos shouting about veganism, or motor maintenance or the need to restore Pooh Bear to his former glory: the Societies' Fair is in full flood. At least, that's what my scrunched-up information sheet says; it feels more like an attempt on the split-an-eardrum, stamp-on-a-foot world records. Smells – sweat and fags – are almost tangible (and by the way, how on earth did they manage to light their fags? I've had seven elbow-crushed!). Sights are blurred – I'm too scared to actually focus on anything – anyway, if I can't see, perhaps I'm not really here.

Escape is vital. Can't reach the doors, they're jammed. Get away from the stalls, quick. End up crushed in the middle of the room; here are all the other idiots who've tried the Houdini bit.

Thinking about it, the whole Fair is rather ridiculous. After all, who really cares whether you join a particular society at a particular time on a particular day? You'll find out about them soon enough anyway; they plaster their posters over every wall! In fact, even if you are attracted by any club during this Fair, it might be better to hang on before you do join, until you know when you have free time.

For the first weeks, most freshers have their work cut out just surviving, and most societies will be there all year. It's a shame that such rational thoughts don't come easily when you're still in the midst of the mob, wondering whether the quickest escape would be by digging a tunnel.

Registration

Then there's registration, where you feel like a criminal because your surname has a common initial; if it had begun with "Z" you'd have been in a queue a tenth of the length, without that monstrous registrar at the head of it. You're far too bewildered to appease or put down the officious staff.

Some students curl up and wither under this pressure; some get very "loud". You resolve not to befriend that loud, vulgar one – and then hear yourself giggling hysterically too, because you've joined the wrong queue in the first place. In theory, registration time is when you officially join the college; in fact, it's often the time when you see the worst side of college "organisation".

Get-togethers

Later that day, or on another much the same, you'll "get to know" your fellow inmates. On some courses, including the Drama one I took, there's an official get-together, which is useful. Although you might be too self-conscious to enjoy it at the time, you do at least begin to register faces.

Otherwise, these meetings happen in someone's room – usually the one who was even louder than you at registration. I have an idea that everyone feels very out-of-it on these occasions (and throughout Freshers' Week); everyone also assumes that others are much more at ease. If you distance yourself from the action, the picture is bleak: the loud ones spout about the day's events; about whom they've met so far; about whom they haven't met; about what they're doing tonight and for the next x weeks, and so on until you know their entire life-story since conception. The silent ones seem not "strong" but screwy at the moment. Gigglers seem impossibly immature; nervous ones possess incredibly irritating twitches. In fact, if you find anyone who seems "normal" in your first few days, either your judgement or their facade is extraordinary.

"Befriending"
You might, however, meet someone who makes you feel secure, when all around is chaos. Watch it! There's probably nothing wrong with that person or with you, but people react in funny-peculiar ways to strange situations. It's unwise, therefore, to indulge your new-found "security" by dressing, eating, drinking identically to your new mate, or by leaping into bed with him or her because you've discovered a friend and FREEDOM! In other words, keep your individuality, without over-emphasising it, and don't pretend to be anyone except yourself.

All this is lies, of course, but only up to a point. You, and hundreds of others, are suddenly living in a new and unfamiliar place, an artificial life in some ways because it is not a microcosm of life outside in any sense. Most students are young; all are considered by the powers-that-be to be intelligent; many are away from home for the first time. In this situation, the majority are torn between elation and uncertainty for the first days at college: there's unspoken competitiveness and too much spoken nonsense. Everyone is aware of this but involved in it; it tends to make most students feel awkward. Just remember that most don't feel "at home" until at least the second term; many want, in fact, to "go home" at the start. During Freshers' Week, tension is at its worst. For example, you might be getting happily plastered in the surprisingly cheap bar, when you suddenly realise that you've just bought drinks for a dozen people you've hardly met. The evening turns completely sour when you remember the huge list of work which tutors gave you earlier that day. The only solution is to progress from merriness to paralysis.

Whatever your feelings, it *is* important to remember that, for most students and tutors, Freshers' Week is an easing-in period after a long holiday. It's there for you to take or leave in any aspect, so don't feel too upset if its "special" events leave you cold.

Having said that, there are many benefits from Freshers' Week. If you are flexible; if you do enjoy discos and beer-swilling contests, noise and fun, forget the tension: just enjoy the week for what it is – a week of introduction, but an untypical week. If you're concerned to meet others on your course, or other Christians, Jews, Muslims, Sikhs; other gays or vegetarians; other Marxists etc., etc., you're likely to get the chance. You'll probably discover the opportunities for enjoying yourself, even if they're not provided at this point.

You'll definitely be able to obtain your NUS card, and that's a valuable object: it gives you the chance to buy cheap Coachcards; to enter theatres, cinemas and concert halls at reduced rates and to take advantage of all other NUS services.

By the end of the week you'll feel a stranger only if you have hibernated, although you're likely still to feel strange. But now, it's time to get down to work!

After Freshers' Week

While Freshers' Week might come as a shock, the following weeks can also be stressful if you're inclined to worry. When I received from tutors a run-down of the first term's work, I returned to my room and started packing. It was only by talking to others who'd reacted similarly, that I laughed instead of leaving. Now is the time when acquaintances may become friends.

You're at an obvious advantage if your subject involves group study, or if you're taught in seminars rather than lectures. Where the teaching is formal, it might demand more effort to find the people with whom you're studying but, especially during the first working week, it's often worth seeking them out: work is often easier if you can share your ideas and problems with others.

To a certain extent, colleges expect you to be slow in the first few weeks, and they cater for this; but even so, you might be expected to assimilate a lot of information in a short time. For the shy ones amongst us, work might become an escape from the "horrors" of the student common rooms and cafes; for others, social life is the escape, while work falls by the wayside. In fact, it's often the ones who forget work when they first arrive who encounter most problems later: to lose the thread now is to lose the basis of study for three years on many courses. If your course is continuously assessed, that's particularly unfunny. Try to start by seeing your priorities and balancing your life accordingly. If work-loads seem horrific, try to realise a) that it's not all to be done at once, and b) that you have been chosen for the course not just because your qualifications have let you in: nowadays, people are selected for their suitability as well as for their intellect. Gain confidence from this.

Loneliness

At this stage, you might lose a hell of a lot of self-respect unnecessarily if you seek "specialist" help. If you have problems, it might be best to talk openly about them. Of course, you might not yet have found friends to talk to. If so, there are many kinds of advisers who can help. Whom you go to depends on the nature of your difficulty, and perhaps on whom you have met so far. But do wait, unless you're desperate, for a week or two to see if your problem will go away. Some sort themselves; some disappear with a bit of self-help: problems occur for most students and the most common, perhaps, arise from loneliness.

Maybe you have one-and-a-half days of formal lectures with people you never see otherwise, and you can't work the rest of the time because you feel you're missing out. First and obvious: remember that everyone misses out on something. Second: do something about your isolation. Misery is addictive if indulged; it feels productive because it's interesting whereas boredom, the initial cause of loneliness, isn't. Unless you have the charm to wallow in self-pity attractively, very little is actually produced by it except a lack of self-respect. If you've never had problems making friends before now, your problems are unlikely to last. If you've never mixed easily with people and are bothered about it, find students on the same course and begin by talking about work. Of course, the opening will be stilted and perhaps uncomfortable, but at least you're talking about a common interest, and things tend to develop from there.

Find cheap activities which seem genuinely attractive. Whenever you feel self-conscious, try to concentrate hard on the *activity*, and not on the people involved. If your course is sedentary, strong physical team activity might help: you'll be so tired after it that you can't do anything but relax.

Drugs

One definite non-cure for loneliness, or any other stress, is artificial escape. Under the heading of "drugs" come cigarettes, booze – even excess tea and coffee if I'm strictly accurate – as well as "illegal substances".

Smoking

As any smoker is aware, *cigarettes* are extremely pricey as well as potentially lethal: unfortunately, that doesn't stop students from taking up the habit nervously or "socially" when they begin college, if they didn't begin behind the bike sheds at school. Whatever the reason for starting to smoke, the majority end up hooked on an upward spiral of puffing. Whilst boozers usually confine their consumption to specific times, smokers take their weed all day, every day: from experience, I know that smokers have to set aside a considerable chunk of grant to be sent up in smoke. Additionally, you have to allow for the fact that you're not the only one who smokes your fags. As a "social" habit, this is one which involves passing the "goodies" round friends, and some friends are more generous in receiving than in giving when it comes to cigarettes. At one stage, when I particularly wanted to make friends, I had to expect to buy a packet of twenty if I wanted to smoke five. So, smoking makes you poorer unless you're a scrounger, in which case it makes you nasty. Smoking also attracts righteous indignation from others who don't want their lungs polluted by your foul addiction (that's fair enough really).

I suppose, in fact, that health reasons are the most sensible to stop – or better, not to start smoking – but as your lungs don't seize up immediately you light up, these may not be as attractive as the feeling of satisfaction you think a fag gives you.

It is satisfying, however, to know that you smell better and tend to be richer when you don't smoke. It's also important to realise that it's easier to give up when *you* decide to, before the bank manager or doctor *tells* you that you must stop; it's least difficult if you think of the positives that might come from saving your fag money.

The Health Education Council, 78 New Oxford Street, London W1A 1AH and *ASH (Action on Smoking and Health)*, 5/11 Mortimer Street, London N1 7RH, have both produced booklets to help you give up smoking; both are government-subsidised. Another non-profit-making organisation (this one, not government-subsidised), is the *NSNS (National Society of Non-Smokers)*, based at Latimer House, 40/48 Hanson Street, London W1P 7DE. The latter is especially helpful to London students: by phoning 01 636 9103, you can arrange to be interviewed by a medical adviser, who is a fully-qualified doctor offering his/her services free of charge. There's also a paperback by Miriam Stoppard called *Quit smoking* (Ariel Books, 1982) which is aimed at individual ways and means of achieving the same end.

Fortunately, society as a whole is veering away from smoking, so it's becoming more common to find very supportive friends to help you.

Booze

Few friends will help you give up booze. As one who would prefer a liquid to solid lunch myself, I'd better watch what I say, in case I get had up for corruption. Actually, there's no doubt that alcohol provides only passing pleasure, and too much at one time leads to that "morning after" feeling, often lasting longer than the fun of the night before. Long-term over-accumulation of booze has well-known disadvantages – both illness and overdrafts. Even so, social drinking is often a large part of college life and, for we weaker vessels, it's not quite the same if you stick to squash.

If you do stick to *moderate* drinking of the cheaper stuff, if you don't miss it when you leave off for a couple of days or feel inclined to booze for breakfast or lunch, you're unlikely to do your health or your pocket terrible harm. Do avoid buying "rounds" however: the more people in the circle, the more likely you are to get paralytic. Also do not drink and drive of course – you're probably finding it hard enough to keep a car on the road (if you have one), without having to pay for the "pleasure" of having it off the road because you've been banned and fined.

In theory, the cheapest booze is home-brewed – and it's not a difficult practice. Be sure that you don't make up for what you've saved on pub money by drinking more of your homemade stuff, which tends to be relatively strong. If you do use pubs or bars you can spend less by arriving later; perhaps do some college work before going out, rather than fooling yourself that you'll work better after a few bevvies.

If you do find that you're relying on alcohol more than simply enjoying it, ring *Alcoholics Anonymous* (under "A" in the phone directory): the people there can help you even before you get to the stage you might consider "alcoholic".

Coffee and tea

Okay, okay; this does sound daft. But caffeine (found mostly in coffee) and tannin (mainly in tea) are another couple of legal drugs which you're likely to meet regularly. Both are stimulants, as opposed to alcohol which relaxes, and both are unhealthy if taken in excess. If you find trouble sleeping or concentrating, count how many mugs of coffee (particularly) you down daily, before you label yourself an insomniac: drinking less tea or coffee might be a very simple remedy for a really irritating affliction.

Illegal drugs

Irritation, afflictions, stress or plain spirit of adventure often lead people from the legal to the illegal drug scene. At the moment, at lot is spoken, written and shrieked about the nature of illegal drugs and their harmfulness or otherwise. The first thing to remember is that the thrill of consuming "illicit" substances can easily be dulled by being caught and having to pay a fine or worse. But there are varying degrees of danger, criminal and physical, associated with particular drugs: here's a run-down.

Cannabis/grass is the most widely used drug, the one that many campaign to have legalised. Many "authorities" accept that cannabis itself does little harm, but the "joint" – its usual form of consumption – usually contains tobacco, which *is* harmful, so don't kid yourself that cannabis-smoking is entirely harmless. And although cannabis isn't addictive, the tobacco content is. The effect of cannabis is to slow down the body's metabolism (relaxing body and mind) which can lead, in hardened smokers, to lethargy and fat. Penalties for possessing cannabis vary from area to area, but the first offence is usually dealt with by a "small" fine. If you're found growing or dealing, you'll probably receive a large fine or even, after the first offence, a prison sentence.

If you're found to possess or deal in more dangerous drugs, the "A1" drugs, it's quite on the cards that you'll be chucked into jail straight away, which won't increase your chances of gaining a degree or later, a job. As important as this, is the health hazard associated with these drugs.

■ *Amphetamines (speed)* come in several forms. *Sulphate* the most common, is an A1 drug which comes in the form of a white powder: other amphetamines come in pill-form. As you might expect, speed increases the metabolism, and may give you heightened, frenzied alertness and energy, as well as a reduced appetite. If it's taken in quantity over a time, it can cause depression, irritability and weight loss, as well as general physical weakness. It can also be addictive, particularly if injected.

■ *LSD (Acid)* has been attributed a mystical quality. In fact, it is

hallucinatory, altering the user's perception of reality. It can be
very dangerous to those who are mentally or emotionally
unstable, or even to anyone who takes it when in a bad mood.
Acid is an A1 drug. "Magic mushrooms", which grow wild,
have similar effects to Acid and are also illegal.

■ *Heroin (or Diamorphine; also known as "horse" or "H")*: very much
in the news, widely available and addictive, heroin is a
desperately slow way of committing suicide. It's used by
doctors to relieve immense pain; it shouldn't be used, I reckon,
for any other reason.

■ *Cocaine (or Coke)*: once upon a time cocaine was used as a local
anaesthetic; now it isn't. It's not physically addictive, but you
won't know that once you've become psychologically hooked,
psychologically and physically damaged. Be warned!

One last word on illegal drugs. Many people who take them do so
at first, to escape from stress. In fact, at the risk of trying to sound
profound, I might say that those people are really trying to escape
from themselves: their answer won't be in drugs, which reduce
rather than offer freedom and independence. There's nothing
romantic in taking drugs for any reason, particularly since the stress
caused as a result of drug-taking might make your earlier problems
seem piddling. Even cannabis, though not addictive in itself, might
put into your mind the idea of "experimenting" with harder stuff
which really is dangerous. If you do get into the drugs scene and
encounter problems, contact *Release*, 1 Elgin Avenue, London W9
(Tel: 01 289 1123), who will also help with any legal difficulties
you've got into.

Coping with study

Sometimes, people only realise that their true problems are
associated with work when they've gone through the dangerous
"escapes" from it. Far more clever is to realise, straight away, that
work is the first problem to face positively. It's almost always
threatened if you're tense. Instead of indulging in worry or

"escape", *do* some work – even when you think what you're doing is rubbish: for many, the only way to fail a course is by failing to hand in assignments.

If you're not motivated by the work, still do it. Find an aspect which does interest you, if you can; if not, persist while you're searching for stimulus. Suss out why you're finding it heavy-going, and discover whether it's your problem or the course's. It might be nothing more than the fact that you haven't learnt to study in the way that's expected. "A" levels are almost always an advanced form of memory test – not so relevant to colleges as the entry requirements might suggest. Instead, college courses encourage you to support your reading with your own ideas. You're expected to rely much more upon your own resources, than to depend upon books to do all your work. Interest, argument and questioning are often more important than rote-learned facts; reading the "key" points is better than reading cover-to-cover.

Sympathetic tutors will offer you ideas of how to train yourself, and they'd far rather you approached them early in the year than later, when you might have no chance of catching up.

If, when you've talked about your difficulties and have given the course a good try, you still hate it, see if there's another course in the same establishment which interests you. You can transfer courses by talking to heads of your old and new departments, if both have a clear idea of your ultimate aims and present objectives. It's more difficult to change college, or to leave altogether, especially after the first term.

If you leave on medical grounds (or make a straight transfer), you should be okay. If, however, you leave for other reasons after a term or more of one three-year course, you might have to return any grant money you've received. It will also spoil your chances of being financed for another full course. So, leaving is quite a big step to take officially: if you're seriously thinking of taking it, do talk to a tutor and/or counsellor first.

At the other end of the spectrum is wanting to stay at college when you may not be able to. If this is due to lack of work, or poor work, you'll probably be given a warning before you're kicked out.

Don't ignore it; respond by talking to the person who's warned you, and try to work out together ways of bucking up.

Sex

Contraception

If you're sleeping with someone of the opposite sex, take precautions against pregnancy – don't leave it to your friend. Men can obtain these easily: women often have to go to a doctor. The college doctor should prescribe contraceptives, either to avoid pregnancy or to alleviate period pains.

If you or your friend does become pregnant, I'd advise speaking to NUS people and/or doctors first – those who are least likely to involve value judgement in their talk.

■ The *pill* comes in two forms: the combined pill, containing oestrogen and progestogen, which stop ovulation; and the mini pill, which has only progestogen. The combined pill has to be taken regularly, with some leeway allowed. The mini pill must be taken daily at the same time, and never more than three hours' late. Instead of stopping ovulation, it shakes things up, making it difficult for the sperm to settle, or for the womb to accept a fertilized egg.

   Apart from being the most effective contraceptive (98–100% effective), the pill is easy to use. It regulates periods, and often causes reduced pre-menstrual tension, pain and bleeding. On the minus side, a few women get depressed by the pill. It also might be unsuitable if you smoke heavily or have high blood pressure, diabetes or heart trouble; enquire carefully before settling for it. Risks of side-effects are said to be increased if you're under 21 years of age and, to be honest, not a great deal is known about its long-term side-effects in any case.

   Remember that the pill does not work if it's taken more than twelve hours' late, or when you have sickness or diarrhoea.

■ The *intrauterine device*, more familiar to us plebs as "the coil", also has two varieties: IUD and IUDC. With either, you're 96–98%

protected, but it is not so suitable if you've never been pregnant before. The coil is a small plastic or plastic and copper device which works by stopping an egg fertilizing. It has to be inserted by a doctor and is effective for two-three years. It might cause heavier menstrual bleeding and, especially if you sleep with several partners, a pelvic infection. It's also possible that the IUD will come out.

■ The *diaphragm* or *cap* is 97% effective, assuming you're careful. It's got to be used with a spermicide which can be obtained from chemists. The cap is a soft rubber device which you insert in the vagina before intercourse to cover the womb entrance: this prevents any sperm ever meeting an egg. It must be left in place for six hours after intercourse. If you gain or lose weight, have the cap checked – in other words, only if the cap fits, wear it!

The *condom* is 97% effective but, as with the cap, should be used with a spermicide. Remember, men, that it is the easiest contraceptive to acquire. It's made of rubber and is worn over the erect penis. It works only when used properly, so read the instructions!

■ The *"safe period"* is used, usually, only by those with religious or ethical objections to other forms of contraception. Its effectiveness is rather hit-and-miss (excuse the expression), but it must be better than nothing.

The method relies on no device, but the woman must record daily her body temperature, noting the changes in vaginal mucus, and then must avoid sex during what she has worked out to be her most fertile period. A doctor will give more details, but note that, if you have irregular periods, this method is very unreliable.

■ The *"day-after" pill* is a relatively new device which can be taken after intercourse, if prescribed by a doctor. It means that you must get to a doctor pretty soon after sex: you're prescribed a pill to take two or three times; which is almost totally effective. If – by a strange quirk – it's not, you're almost forced to have an abortion (not always on the NHS) because the baby is likely to be very deformed. The "day-after" pill is a massive dose of

ingredients contained in the ordinary pill; its long-term
side-effects aren't fully known, but no-one has recommended its
regular use.

Abortion

If you do get pregnant and don't want to go through with the
pregnancy, you can find out from your doctor or (less
traumatically, perhaps) from Brook Advisory Centres (Central
Clinic, 233 Tottenham Court Road, London W1) or from others
(see *Useful addresses* at the end of this guide), whether you're entitled
to a free abortion. I'd suggest that conventional contraceptives are
better than this: abortions are often traumatic; the preliminaries are
also complicated by the law which says that you can only have an
abortion (NHS or paying) if you're likely to be physically or
psychologically harmed if you go through with the pregnancy.

Sleeping with your own sex

If you've read the previous section, you might even be feeling
fortunate that you're attracted to your own sex. If, on the other
hand, you're a bit screwed up by your discovery, try not to let it
override the rest of your life, immense though it may seem.

Although male homosexuality under twenty-one is still officially
illegal, virtually no-one at college will bother you with that
information, if you don't bother them. I think that college gays are,
in fact, some of the luckiest – male or female. Most students (and the
more enlightened lecturers) take people for who they are rather than
for the box that others might put them in.

If you're worried about finding yourself to be gay, decide
whether you can talk to friends, first; then perhaps, to the NUS at
your college, which might give you contacts. Otherwise, you
might contact *CHE (Campaign for Homosexual Equality)*,
BM/CHE, London WC1N 3XX: it's a campaigning group, but has
people aware of your situation. There's also the *Gay Youth
Movement*, BM/GYM, London WC1N 3XX, to which you could
write. Other addresses are to be found in the *Useful addresses* section
at the end of this guide.

Above all, remember that you're neither a freak nor a "special case" simply because you're gay: your personality need not change because of your discovery; neither need your response to others generally. Of course, get to know other gays as and when you can – they can help and support you – but don't encase yourself in a world which has only a negative relationship with heterosexuals. Heterosexual gossip does abound and can irritate: it's still a part of the society to which you belong. I reckon that this is the time and place to see and accept yourself within that society, because there's still a lot in it that caters for you.

Venereal disease
The illness that you always believe you'll never get. You are unlikely to get it, of course, but nevertheless, about 250 people each week under the age of twenty, do begin treatment for VD.

The two most common types are *gonorrhea* and *syphilis*; both are caught most frequently by having sex with someone who has the illness; both are most easily treated if diagnosed quickly.

The symptoms of gonorrhea, for women, might be: unusual vaginal discharge, a burning sensation when urinating, fever, chill and stomach pains. Men might also feel pain when urinating and/or have a yellow discharge from the penis.

The more difficult to spot, but also the most serious if left, is syphilis. Symptoms may take up to three months to appear, and even then, may not be painful. The primary symptoms can be painless sores on the sex organs, which later turn into ulcers. There may also be mouth sores, body rashes, lumps and flu-like symptoms. The most deceptive thing about syphilis is that the symptoms often disappear after a few weeks; and then, the disease is most dangerous.

If you suspect that you have VD of any type, go to your local doctor or hospital clinic; your case will be treated in confidence. Both are very easily treated if discovered in their early stages; both are unpleasant later.

Cystitis

Women are as likely to have cystitis as VD (some of the symptoms are similar) but cystitis is not sexually transmitted: it is, however, a cause of pain when urinating. You should be able to cure cystitis by drinking a heck of a lot of water containing a pinch of sodium bicarbonate (baking soda); but if you're still worried after this hasn't worked, do go to a doctor or the local hospital clinic.

The law

If you get into trouble with the police (it *is* possible), it's useful to know your basic legal rights.

Apart from giving your name and address, you don't have to say a thing to police who question you. However, it's a good idea to co-operate, especially if the questions are harmless.

You can be searched without a warrant for drugs, firearms and stolen property, but the police must give you a reason for the search if they're asked. They can take anything which they believe might be useful to them, but you're allowed to ask for a receipt and for the return of any legitimate article in what is called "due course".

If the police ask to search you, it's best not to refuse: that action in itself might get you taken to a police station, searched there and charged with "obstructing a police officer in the course of his/her duty . . . " But do make a note of the reason you're given for the search; also ask for some identification, and for the police officer's number. Later on, you can make an official complaint, if you think you've been treated wrongly.

Arrest

You can be arrested without a police warrant for dozens of offences, including:

- breach of the peace
- refusing, or failing, a breath test
- theft
- possession of an offensive weapon.

As with being searched, make sure you're given a reason for being arrested; remember what is said (if you can't write it down) and remember the officer's number. Again, "go peacefully" if you don't want to be charged with obstruction, and raise any objections later.

At the police station, you'll be asked to answer questions and to make a statement – if you're going to be charged. Make sure you know exactly what you're being charged with first of all, then answer questions if you wish – you don't have to.

Before making a statement, you can ask for legal aid which should be free to you as a student. The police aren't obliged to allow this but if they refuse, they've got to note down that fact and the reason for it. They *do* have to give you writing materials, if you ask for them.

If the police don't charge you, you should be released within twenty-four hours. If they do, they must either release you on bail, or bring you to a Magistrates' Court within that time (or by Monday, if you're held over the weekend).

Help and advice

For other problems which are less "boxable", but which really do need an expert ear, there are several types of ear you can bend. Broadly, they come under three categories: all are "professional" in some way, and should treat all you tell them in confidence. It'll help you and your adviser if you treat him/her not as the friend you might want, but simply as a knowledgeable person who is helping you: the adviser should never become *part* of your problems!

Tutors/lecturers

Tutors and lecturers are most likely to know you and your general situation. They are "in the know" about courses; they also have access to reports and references concerning you (be prepared for them to think they understand you better than they actually do; just as you might judge people from the sides you see of them). Possibly the most helpful concerning work and its problems, tutors might be less "wordly-wise" than other advisers.

Counsellors

Counsellors may be employed by the college or by the NUS. They
are trained to deal with all sorts of difficulties, and are likely to have
contacts if you need further help. Problem-solving with a
counsellor is through conversation, not medication: that might
prevent you from visiting a doctor for a valium fix, which can't be
bad!

College doctors

College doctors don't *always* treat patients with a prescription. If
yours does, tread carefully; you're not really going to be helped by
becoming drug-dependent. Many college doctors are sympathetic
and broad-minded, but not all. You can change your doctor if you
want a second opinion.

   Whatever his/her personal stance, any doctor (or other
"outsider") can only interpret your situation from what you say of
it. This might be very useful if you've become immersed in
difficulties which you should be distanced from. For physical
problems a doctor is almost always the best person to visit first: if
you disagree with his/her advice, by all means find others – but your
problems only become "official" (if necessary), when you've
visited a qualified doctor.

Telephone "help lines"

Aside from the formal channels of advice, there's often a telephone
"help line" run by students. This provides many of the services
offered by other advisers, with the added advantage (or
disadvantage, depending on you and your problem) of student
counsellors. Most students have seen college from roughly the
same angle as you, even if specific degrees of approach differ.

Parents

Consulting parents about problems is, for many, a dodgy matter.
I'm generalising when I say that parents cannot understand the
particular pressures of college, but some don't and, for these, your
difficulties in "settling in" or whatever, might be upsetting. A

college problem might be exacerbated by over-protective parents, or by those who dismiss your worries: rarely can parents actually do anything to help.

However, I think it is worth talking to friends and fellow students about most problems first. Remember that, whoever talks out your difficulties with you is an individual whom you may or may not "get on with". If one adviser isn't suitable, don't despair; find someone who does seem more sympathetic to you.

Making a bit on the side

The words "student" and "poor" are almost synonymous; your relative poverty will be constant while you study. But – if you're used to a higher standard of living, or if you *want* a higher standard of living, or simply, if you want a holiday – there is action you can take, without robbing the local bank.

Tax

One benefit of your financial poverty as a student is that you don't earn enough, purely on grant "earnings", to qualify for tax. The grant does count as earnings toward the tax threshold, but there are a few hundred pounds between the usual grant allowance and the amount you have to earn before tax applies. So all you earn, if you're lucky enough to find a job, is likely to be yours, except for the National Insurance deduction which isn't terrific.

Apart from the obvious financial advantage of work, there's an added bonus: when you leave college, any curriculum vitae which includes a list of jobs as well as a run-down of academic achievements is likely to impress prospective employers.

Holiday work

Holiday work is hard to come by at the moment, but don't let this put you off; just apply very early. If you write in by September, you might still be able to get sorting or delivery work with the GPO at Christmas; they always need extra staff at that time, and it's often a case of first come, first served. They do discriminate in that they're more likely to accept applicants who have filled in their forms not only legibly, but also neatly (and that applies for most jobs). They also give preference to students who've worked for them before, so when you've once got in the door, you might be set up for three years.

Again, as with all jobs, you might need a curriculum vitae which should be typed, informative and succinct. For any interview, wear "nice" clothes and make sure your fingernails are clean!

During the summer holiday, when you've only a choice between a job or the dole, there are more varied prospects.

Some factories and big stores take on students to replace the regulars who are on holidays. As with any job, you've got to apply a long way ahead to be in with a chance. Along with the work, there often goes some antagonism from the regular staff; with factory work there's almost always boredom to cope with too, but you're only doing for a month or two what many do for life – and you rarely have to concentrate so hard that you can't think about other things.

You might also apply – EARLY (in case you haven't had that rammed down enough!) – for jobs with the local council; you could be anything from a roadsweeper to a playscheme leader, and pay is reasonable. You could be a hospital porter: for that, apply to local hospitals.

People in large cities can often make a packet by temp typing which, because of the variety of places you find yourself in, can be quite interesting.

For holiday work not mentioned here, contact your local *Manpower* office (under "M" in the phone directory) which, despite its name, caters for both sexes. Otherwise, trundle round likely spots and offer your services politely and charmingly!

Working abroad

If you want more adventurous work (in theory, at least), you may have to accept much lower pay. There are opportunities for fruit-picking in Britain and Europe, where hours tend to be very long as well as poorly paid, but it could be fun to live with other

students for a month or two in "foreign parts" – and if you're
picking grapes, you can get sloshed every night, very cheaply! For
specific jobs in greater detail, contact *Vacation Work International*, 9,
Park End Street, Oxford (Tel: 0865 41976); or *PGL Sunsport
Holidays*, Station Street, Ross-on-Wye, Herefordshire (Tel: 0989
4212): the latter specialise in the south of France.

Opportunities in the USA are provided by *Bunac*, 30, Store
Street, London WC1 (Tel: 01 637 7686) or *Camp America*, 37,
Queen's Gate, London SW7 (Tel: 01 589 3223). Again, the old story
of low pay, but it is the USA!

The first American scheme, offered by both companies, gives
you your return fare, pocket money plus a live-in job for two
months or so. Work is in a kids' summer camp where you'll be
supervising "activities" – you've clearly more chance of getting on
these schemes if you're taking a teaching course, or a practical,
perhaps "arty" course. After finishing the job, most students
remain for a holiday, but that comes largely out of your own pocket.

The work demands stamina and enterprise, as well as resistance
to, or enjoyment of, American accents! From what I hear, a heck of
a lot is expected of you in these places; a heck of a lot is learnt, too!

Bunac has a second scheme for getting to the USA, but you need
contacts and some of your own money for this: they arrange for a
three-month work permit and, if you want, a job list. Then, after
you've paid registration fees and fares, America is your oyster.

Term work

If you can *type* and own a typewriter, you might be onto a winner
without leaving your room. Some colleges demand that all essays,
dissertations, theses, etc., are typed: some professionals charge vast
sums for the service. You can charge much less and still make
money; but do make sure that you've sussed out the required
lay-out, and that your mistakes aren't too devastating!

You can *cut hair*? Again, you've a ready market of students: the
work can really take off if satisfied customers are willing to praise
your talents on the grapevine. If, on the other hand, you need a
haircut and don't know anyone to do it, try either hairdressing

schools (which are usually inexpensive), technical colleges with hairdressing courses (which might be free) or smaller hairdressers (where new assistants are trained "on the job").

Sewing and *knitting* are also skills which can prove lucrative, particularly if you make clothes cheaper than they are in the shops. Admittedly, you'll be hard-pressed to undercut second-hand shops and markets; if that is so, work hard on your designs to ensure true originals.

If you own a car or motorbike, enquire about *mini-cab* work or *messenger riding*: if you're an ace mechanic, advertise the fact around college.

Actually, any skill you have can be turned to profit (doesn't that sound mercenary?), if you're prepared to charge reasonable to low rates, and if you have the time to give a good service.

All the aforementioned term work can be done as and when you like. If your college course runs only during office hours, you've a wider choice of casual work.

Try *bar work* or working in a *restaurant*; you might even find a job in a *late-night shop* or in one that takes *Saturday staff*.

Determination to be employed is the first step to getting work – although you'll still have to work hard to find one. Don't give up with the first, or even thirtieth, rejection and don't let prospective employers know by your attitude that you've been rejected before. As a final summing up, a few tips about applying:

■ *application forms* should be filled in neatly and concisely. Rather than crush all your achievements into the meagre space offered, use a separate page to answer questions, but don't be unnecessarily long-winded.

■ *curriculum vitae* should be typed and, again, concise. They should include your name; address; date of birth; places of education (since the age of 11); previous work – paid and voluntary; special "talents" such as driving, and the names of two referees.

■ *interviews* are horrible! Dress in a way that you reckon suits the place; make sure you're clean down to your fingernails, and smile! Whatever the work, give the impression you want it.

Benefits

If you can't get a job, you are eligible for *supplementary benefit* from the DHSS (or *unemployment benefit* if you've worked before for a time) – but only during the summer holiday.

First, register at the local Social Security office as unemployed and available for work. You generally receive your first Giro cheque the day after you first sign on.

For single parents and disabled students the procedure is different: you should apply directly to the DHSS offices.

The only students who should be careful in claiming are those from overseas: you run the risk of having your whole situation re-assessed if you apply for any benefit, so first take advice.

Holidays

Once you've amassed your fortune in the first part of summer (or whenever), take advantage of the many student concessions offered to have a holiday.

Planes, boats, trains – and coaches

Apart from Rail and Coachcards in Britain (obtainable from the appropriate stations), there's the *Inter-Rail Card*, available from main railway stations. The outlay for this is quite high, but it does allow you to travel in Europe, Scandinavia and Morocco by rail *free*, for a month. You're also entitled to half-price Sealink and B & I shipping tickets with the card. Travelling by boat, save some cash for the duty-free goods!

If you're flying off, and can book three months' ahead, try *Apex (Advanced Purchased Excursion)* tickets, which offer scheduled return flights much more cheaply than with later bookings. Otherwise, hunt round *bucket shops*, which sell off the airlines' left-overs. Look out for cheap flights advertised in *The Guardian, The Times* and (in London) *Time Out*.

Do-it-yourself

Hitching is the cheapest form of long-distance travel. It can also be very hazardous; less so if you take vital precautions. You're more likely to get a lift in the first place if you look "respectable", have a light luggage pack and a notice stating where you want to be. In Britain, a "please" added to the notice has helped me in the past. Wherever you are, have some warm clothes, light-coloured or fluorescent, and waterproofs: hypothermia takes the pleasure out of hitching.

Once you get into the car, lorry, agricultural vehicle or whatever, keep awake! Be polite to the driver, and try to keep off controversial subjects, unless you're cunning enough to agree with what's said. Where you sense difficulties arising, act as undisturbed as possible, and keep chatting. According to my ex-lorry driver brother who's full of "trucking" stories, a hitcher is less likely to be hassled in any way if he/she makes the driver laugh – so have ready a store of funny, non-risky jokes.

If the worst comes to the worst, and you're truly terrified, you could make out that you've just discovered you're on the wrong road, or on the wrong side of it (though this will take some acting ability, if you've displayed the destination notice). Don't do anything to disable the driver, or you might both be for it.

Cycling is also a cheap form of travel, but it might become problematic when you want to cheat a few miles on the train – especially in Britain. A few services on every route allow bikes to travel free, but on others they're forbidden or charged for; so check with British Rail before you turn up at a station with your bike.

Car trips are cheap only if there's a group of people travelling and sharing costs; but then they are cheap and, of course, very convenient. On very long journeys, don't overload so much that people are sardined out of all comfort.

Passports

Obviously, the first thing to do when you think of travelling abroad is to make sure you've a valid passport. You can buy a year's one (only accepted in some countries but including EEC countries) at post offices, which has the benefit of "instant" service, the disadvantage of being relatively pricey in the long run. For five or ten-year passports, you must allow *at least* a month for the paper work. Either go to the post office for an application form and send it to Clive House, 70–78 Petty France, London S.W.1, or apply directly to Petty France. If you actually go there with everything that is required, you should be able to get a passport the same day as long as you are prepared to wait.

Visas
For many countries outside western Europe, you'll need a visa. Information about these can be obtained from your local Passport Office or the relevant embassy. Again, remember the bureaucracy takes time.

Immunisation
Be prepared for jabs if you're travelling to Africa, Asia or Latin America and allow at least three weeks for them to "take" before you go. Your doctor will be able to innoculate you against most diseases, and should refer you to an immunisation centre for the rarer jabs. Addresses of these centres can also be found in the International Certificate of Vaccination booklet, in which your vaccination must be noted.

Money
Travellers' cheques are the least nickable form of money and can be obtained from your usual bank, but take some local currency too, in case you can't cash a cheque immediately you arrive. Also find a secure place to conceal your money and passport. You can buy wallets which tie round your waist under your clothes: some are supposed to be waterproof, but I have a mangled passport which proves that this theory doesn't always hold.

Luggage
Label all luggage with your name and address, and also the address to which you're travelling if this is practicable. Obviously, the less you take, the less you have to lose as well as the less to carry.

Finally, read all the blurb from any travel agent/holiday firm you use. Not only is their advice valuable – because they should know the holidays they're dealing with – but so is the "small print", which tells you your rights, or lack of them. If the blurb says nothing about insurance, ask about it – and don't leave until you have some cover.

Remember that, as a student, you have long holidays and many concessions on travel: get your travelling in now, if you possibly can.

3. Successful skimping

Setting yourself up ■ household tips ■
grow it yourself ■ washing clothes ■
simple sewing ■ heating ■ coping with
electricity ■ shopping

Setting yourself up

My God!! Suddenly you get no meals unless you buy them or cook
them yourself! Actually, setting yourself up, especially if you're
"self-catering", has novelty value at first: it can provide hours of
long-term fun too, if you get organised.

You may have to fit your life around a timetable; you may have to
give yourself a routine. The sooner you suss out what you have to
do and when, the freer and more relaxed you'll be: ironic, isn't it?

Apart from expecting you to attend sessions at college, no-one is
going to tell you when to work: the trouble is, they do set deadlines
by which the assignments have to be done. Some courses demand
regular tutorials to ensure you're working continuously, and to
help you along the way. If you work best under the pressure of
tomorrow's deadline, and resent being "checked up on", such a
system might seem a pain in the proverbials; but it is a great safety
net for those who *think* they work best under pressure, without
realising the mass of continuous study involved. So I reckon that if
you're given the chance of tutorials, you should take it.

If you're expected to work alone, the routine you give yourself
must be fairly strict – though totally personal. Do you know at what
time of day you work best?, when you're fit for nothing but
collapsing?, when you most enjoy food? Can you suss out where
you work best? Without giving yourself an hourly timetable (unless
that's what you're into) and, perhaps without even testing your
metabolic rate, try to divide your days so that you have the time and
inclination to work, rest and play – without the Mars Bar!

Household tips

You've probably washed up before, but can you do it economically? Can you wash clothes by hand so that they remain the same size? Do you know one end of a sewing needle or a plug from the other? Will you have access to an iron and, if not, can you dry clothes so that they bear no relation to mangled dishclothes? If you do have an iron, can you use it?

These skills, and others, can be picked up from the usual household slave in your family before you get to college. They're called chores only because they're regular tasks: they *can* be enjoyed, and certainly they make a change from poring over books. They're also exercise – separate from the other one of lifting the beer glass – and any form of exercise is healthy for mind and body. The art of housework is getting into a habit of doing it quickly: here are a few tips.

■ First, find *a space for everything*. Whatever the size of the space you live in, this is important; if you live with others, it's vital. The idea won't seem so daft when you've just ripped your only posh trousers as you're going out in them and you can't find the sticky tape, let alone a needle and thread. You tend to waste money as well as time when you lose things, by buying what you already have.

   Certain chain-stores sell plastic "organiser" boxes with twenty or so compartments. Ostensibly for the "handyman", they're also very convenient for anyone who wants to keep tabs on their pins, fuses, paper clips etc.

■ Once you're fairly organised, you can become a prize hoarder of "rubbish". As long as you're not mightily extreme, the habit can be a source of great satisfaction (not to say smugness) to the poor.

■ For example, old *newspapers* are marvellous for covering anything about to get messy; for wrapping vegetable peelings (if you don't use them for soup!); for papier maché presents; for cutting out letters to make greetings cards etc.

■ Other *paper*, which you've used on one side only, is good for shopping lists and notes. Keep all scraps together in a particular place where everyone can find them. You could also use them to make a list of anything lent or borrowed outside the house. Keep all borrowed bits together: otherwise, library books, especially, tend to hide when they're most needed.

■ Keep *old washing-up liquid bottles* to squirt alien species off your plants (they're often more effective with some of the soap still in); or to squirt anyone who annoys you during Rag Week. Actually most *used and lidded containers* are handy to store something in.

■ Before you re-cycle any "empties", make sure they *are* empty.

■ When bottles of deodorant, shampoo, sauce are running out, store them upside-down. If the contents dilute, swish some water around in them on their last "serving".

■ Keep those irritating ends of soap to weld together when you've enough to make a new one – a soap-box can be an effective mould.

■ If you live with others, devise a *weekly kitty* for essentials. Use it to take advantage of *stamps* sold by gas and electricity showrooms. Buy them regularly and stick them on the card provided, which you send off when you receive a bill. It only *seems* cheaper to pay this way, but it certainly spreads out the cost.

■ You can also buy *telephone stamps* in the same way, from post offices, but it might be better to pay for these from a box by the phone, where people can put money when they make calls. Put a telephone charges book with the box, and try to find a box with a key so that the money-flow doesn't proceed the wrong way.

■ You might eat together often enough to make a general *food kitty* worthwhile.

■ For "group" shopping, keep a permanent *shopping list* and add to it items which are running out; cross out each thing as it's bought

■ It's also an idea to have a *rota* among residents for the dreaded *housework*. You could either take a set of jobs in turn, or a set of days. While you may not have noticed housework being done in the past, it's quite important: hovels breed horrible stuff like illness, mice etc., which are more difficult to clear up than a spot of dust (to be fair, you can acquire mice if you're completely sanitised – if you are plagued, the local council will supply you with pellets, without cost).

Grow it yourself

From cleaning to catering, it's d.i.y. from now on. You can even go to the extremes, if you're really eager, and grow it yourself.

Growing certain foods is cheap, convenient and decorative. If you've never done it before, gain confidence by starting small. Try tipping some *mustard and cress seed* onto saturated blotting paper, cotton wool or flannel: *bean sprouts* work on almost the same principle, and are a bit more exotic.

Progress to herbs: *chives, parsley* and *mint* are kids' play: in fact, most herb plants can be bought cheaply and are usually worth their salt(!). *Sage, marjoram* and other similar herbs are quite easily grown on window-sills.

You can *store* herbs by picking the leaves just before they flower, drying them thoroughly in a warm place, and shoving them in airtight jars.

If your success in this "field" sparks you onto greater ideas, there are many possibilities of growing veg; as long as you stay in one place long enough to reap your harvest.

Runner beans grow virtually anywhere (but they need watering in summer, so don't try them unless you'll be around then); *cabbage, lettuce* and *greens* are also almost foolproof.

Washing clothes

Washing clothes *by hand* isn't difficult, but it is laborious. Try to do the maximum amount in one go to save on hot water, and do the whites first when the water is hottest and cleanest. Don't overdo the suds, or you'll have to spend hours rinsing: lack of rinsing causes itching.

However you wash your clothes, if you want them to survive, follow the instructions on their labels and on the powder packet.

Machine washing
Most of the work is done for you by a machine, but only if you recognise the symbols on clothes:

is for very hot washes – white cotton and linen.

is for coloured cotton and linen – the stuff that *doesn't* run.

for nylons, polyester/cotton mixtures.

for coloured versions of the above.

is a warm wash for cotton, linen, rayon etc., where the colours would run at a higher temperature.

acrylics, mixtures of wool and man-made stuff.

for wool – a cool wash.

I'd wash wool by hand in any case: the convenience of the machine suddenly pales when your grandma sees you in her painstaking handiwork, now several sizes too small.

Drying clothes
Jumpers can also grow: this happens when you hang them up to dry. Instead, wrap them in towels until they're beyond the dripping stage, then put them in a warm place.

Other clothes, which don't stretch, are best hung dripping wet; but only if they're not going to drip onto a posh carpet. As they dry, creases tend to drop out, making ironing less vital. If you're lucky enough to have access to a *drier*, fold the clothes loosely as they go in and don't chuck in too many at a time.

Ironing
Yeuch!! (You might enjoy it!) I suppose that ironing's best done when you want to listen to a record or the radio.

If you can store ironed clothes so that they don't re-crease, iron loads at once, because you can work a system that uses the minimum of electricity. Iron the more delicate stuff when the temperature is cool.

Symbols on clothes' labels depicting heat-strengths are:

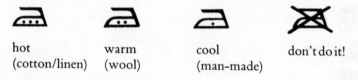

| hot | warm | cool | don't do it! |
| (cotton/linen) | (wool) | (man-made) | |

If you have an iron but no board, spread several thickness of sheet (or something similar) between the flat surface you're using and the material to be ironed: this prevents nasty scorching on tables, holes in carpets, melted plastic, burnt homes etc.

Very dry clothes should be splashed with water before ironing (unless you have a steam-iron which does it for you), or done with a damp cloth between the material and the iron. If you're worried about some expensive fabric, use the latter method in any case.

Finally, be sure that any clothes are not at all damp when you put them away, or they might go mouldy!

Stain removing

Like most things, the sooner stains are tackled the better your chance of success.

Almost always, you can do no harm – and often some good – by rinsing or sponging a stain with cold water. Otherwise, there's actually a "miracle" cure for most stains; unfortunately you can't rinse the material first, because it has to be dry when you use "*Swarfega*". This is a green jelly, which can be used on skin, too. Rub the stuff in and leave for a few hours; then rinse in warm water: it works on almost everything from coffee to grease.

Another good stain remover is *salt*; it works particularly well on fruit stains, including wine. Rub in the salt, then stretch the material over a bowl. Pour boiling water through, and repeat if necessary: often, there's no need.

Other than that, check the following list for other major stain culprits and if the miracle fails, take to the specialist cures:

- *Ball-point pen*: Meths. Rinse afterwards.
- *Beer*: On clothes, try a hot wash, or sponge with 1:5 white vinegar: water.
  On carpets, sponge with warm water.
- *Cigarette burns*: Rub with sandpaper, and then slowly drip a mixture of washing-up liquid and water onto the stain. Rub it over, leave for five minutes and then, if necessary, sponge with a solution of 1 ounce of borax (from chemists) to 1 pint of water. If this seems a huge faff, try scraping the afflicted area with a silver coin.
- *Coffee*: Soapy water.
- *Eye make-up*: Wet the fabric, then use washing-up liquid.
- *Fat*: Scrape it off first, then soak the material in cold water. After that, put it in a hot wash.
- *Gravy*: Wash in warm water.
- *Grass*: Meths. Then rinse.
- *Ink*: "Drown" in cold water. Then use washing-up liquid on the *back* of the stain.

Good luck!

Simple sewing

I'm wondering about the logic of these lists: perhaps failure in removing stains prompts the need for some mending – anyway, don't let's lose the thread(!!?? – I'm only trying to brighten the narrative!).

You'll have to do some mending: try to catch it before the job is serious.

Perhaps you're into making your own clothes: if so, you'll already know a lot more about sewing than I do and might set yourself up as an adviser – this is a guide strictly for the beginner; the one who hardly knows one end of a needle from the other.

Darning

If you have a darning mushroom, the job seems easier. If not, you can use anything which holds the material in place while you're donning the needle – even a hard-boiled egg. Place your "mushroom" under the hole to be mended.

For loosely knitted materials, you can insert a clothes brush where the mushroom would otherwise be; the bristles hold frayed edges in place.

- First, make a circle of running (in-out) stitches about an inch from the edge of the hole; less if the hole is small.
- When that's done, take the thread across the hole in parallel lines.
- Once the hole is covered completely, weave the thread cross-ways across the previous lines, so you've made a warp and weft (to use technical terms). At each end of the line, leave a small loop which allows for the thread to shrink.
- Knot securely, and hope for the best.

Patching

Patching is used for large holes as well as for decoration.

If you're into decorating your clothes, ignore the following and just stitch a square of material onto the right side (the one "they" see) of your cloth. Otherwise:

- Trim the ragged edges of the hole to make a regular shape, preferably a square or rectangle.
- Cut a patch about two inches' larger all round than the hole.
- Assuming you want the patch to be inconspicuous, find a closely matched piece of patch: you can "age" it to suit your faded clothes by soaking it in a solution of soapy water and sodium bicarbonate.
- Tack the patch over the hole on the *wrong* side (the one "they" don't see) of the material, leaving a space of $\frac{1}{2}$–1 inch around the tacking stitches (tacking is a loose in-out stitch which doesn't have to be knotted in place).
- Turn the edges in and stitch properly in place.
- Turn the material to its right side. Finally turn the edges of the

hole in and under, and stitch "invisibly" in place – using matching thread and very small stitches.

Buttons

With buttons, you can't go far wrong by following the holes in the button. Use strong thread, because these attachments take quite a lot of strain. If you're feeling conscientious, put a matchstick between the button and its material but, in any case, don't attach the button too tightly to the material, or you'll have trouble slipping it through the hole.

Torn hems

If possible – from fashion and decency points of view – just raise the hem, which means undoing it with a pin and/or scissors and sewing it up again (see *Taking up a hem*).

   If not, you can use strips of sticky tape for temporary measures (until the next wash), or even staples. Otherwise, the job is complicated and might need an expert.

Ladders

There isn't much you can do to mend ladders, unless they're in thick socks – in that case, treat them like a darn. You can stop them spreading, however, by dabbing the top and bottom of the run with nail polish or soap.

Broken zips

I'm afraid this only refers to zips where the teeth have come out on one side: otherwise, you'll have to find a better seamstress than me.

- Pull the runner to the bottom of the zip.
- With scissors, snip into the detached side of the zip, about $\frac{1}{4}$ inch above it.
- Try to wriggle the teeth above the slit, into the runner: if this doesn't work, try again – and again.
- Pull the runner up.
- Just above your cut, sew firmly (with strong thread) across the zip to make a new bottom.

Replacing elastic
- Cut the elastic to the length of the material, minus about $1\frac{3}{4}$ inches. Attach one end with a safety pin or similar, to the opening.
- Attach the other end to another safety pin (or similar) and push it along inside the tunnel where the elastic should be: you'll need to ruck up the material as you go.
- When the elastic has gone right round, sew it firmly either to itself, or to the other end.
- Sew up the hole.

Taking up a hem
- Measure the length you want your article to be; at about four points round it, to get an even length.
- Pin along the length as a guideline.
- Trim the material to an inch or two below the pin-points. This is really important with flared or tapering material, where the hemline is going to be a different width from the bottom of the material: otherwise, you'll get awful puckers.
- Double-fold (in and in again) the material below the hemline onto the wrong side of the material, using the pin-markers to keep yourself on target.
- Optional for the diligent: press the hemline with an iron; "press" means exactly what it says.
- Carefully over-stitch the wrong side of the hem, using thread close to the colour of the material. Try not to let the stitching show where people notice.
- Iron the lot, placing a damp cloth between the material and the heat, to stop the material marking where you've taken up the hem.

Turning down a hem
This is simpler than it sounds as long as the original hem has enough "spare".
- Unpick the original hem and remove all bits of loose thread.
- Press (with an iron) to get rid of the original crease, using a damp

cloth over the material, and then go on as if you were turning up
a hem.

If there *isn't* enough "spare" material, use *bias binding*, bought from
haberdashers. Bias binding is a strip of material, both edges turned
in towards the middle, on the "wrong" side.

■ Trim the hem edge and lay the binding on it, right sides of the
  material together. Stitch firmly about $\frac{1}{8}$ inch from the edge .
■ Turn it up to the wrong side (inside).
■ Press with an iron.
■ Stitch carefully in place.

Any kind of hemming can be tackled more dramatically with
staples. Sewing connoisseurs may sneer, but for the rest of us, the
idea is useful.

When it comes to more serious sewing (and you were gasping
over this!), you'll either know already more than I do, or you're
interested enough to visit the library for a book. Otherwise, these
basics should help you get by. There might be a friend or
fellow-student you can commission to do more complicated work,
or even to make you clothes for a small fee.

Knitting

For those of you who do a lot of reading, knitting is a productive
hobby to take up at the same time. Buy wool in bulk (and share it
with friends if you're inundated); that's the cheapest way, unless
you're prepared to go through the trouble of unpicking old
jumpers. Luckily for the cack-handed, the simplest articles, like
scarves and tabards are normally the most economical to make
yourself. Do beware of cost if you progress to more ambitious
things: woollies in sales are often cheaper than anything you can
make and, unless you're spectacular with needles, they tend to look
more your size.

Heating

Heating is very expensive: the only really cheap way of keeping
warm is by wearing a lot of clothes (carefully selected to insulate)
and keeping active. If you're intent on keeping fuel bills *very* low or
non-existent, you can take drastic measures in extremely cold
weather: sit with a hot-water bottle, in a sleeping bag or plastic
bin-liner if you're not proud; have a vacuum flask full of hot drink to
ensure the effectiveness. Other, more conventional savings, follow:

- Make your own double-glazing for a song, by fitting clear
plastic sheets to the inside of your windows.
- Close the curtains as soon as it begins to get dark, to keep in any
room-heat from the sun: lighting is cheaper than a bar of the fire.
- Only heat the rooms you're in: heat rises, so the theory is that
you've no need to heat the upstairs rooms. That means, I
suppose, that upper-floor flats don't require heating at all; but
you'd better play that one by ear (if it's frozen, you'll know it
hasn't worked!).

Open fires

Open fires have more going for them than atmosphere: they're also
quite cheap, and very messy. If you can't light yours, it's a bind. The
simplest way is with fire-lighters, which resemble small white
bricks – they're smothered in paraffin – but try not to resort to
undiluted paraffin to get a fire going. Fire-lighters aren't cheap;
they're also considered "amateur" by scout and guide veterans, so
omit them from the following if you're poor, determined and/or
puritanical.

- To lay a fire, start with crumbled fire-lighters; add small twigs,
then coal (the best is old coal which comes from the last fire).
Then, scrunch up balls of paper and chuck them on top.
- Add another layer of coal; scattered rather than solid.
- Check that each layer is evenly distributed; then set fire to every
bit of paper you can see (add a bit more fire-lighter if this doesn't
work).

■ When the flames turn orange, the coal has caught and you've won!

■ Coal pieces fuse after a time. To get them burning merrily, poke the fire.

■ Try to keep the fire in overnight. At the late-night stage, don't poke it, but cover with coal and shut off the air vents beneath the grate. By cutting off the oxygen, you slow the burning process: conversely, if you want a blaze, you can increase oxygen by opening the vents.

■ If you're leaving a fire overnight, or for any length of time, put a fender in front of it to save any sparks from lighting up the room.

■ If your fire has stayed in overnight, open the air vents, rake the ash into the grate and get rid of them. If the fire looks very unhappy, add sugar with more coal to get it going.

■ The conventional method of extinguishing a fire is by closing the air vents and sprinkling it with ashes: if you're desperate, try water.

Gas and paraffin heaters

Gas and paraffin heaters both tend to be easier to light than coal fires, and almost as cheap to run (with calor gas and paraffin, you can easily work out exactly the running costs). However, both forms of heating give off dangerous fumes, especially when the fires are faulty. Ensure that any room housing such heaters is well-ventilated.

Electric fires

Electric fires are cheaper only than storage heaters (which are the bane of many a student's life), but they have the value of being clean and simple to use. If you do have them, close the doors of heated rooms to retain heat, and snuggle round one bar rather than turn on an extra.

Storage heaters

Storage heaters are pricey for what they give you in heat. You have to pay a standing charge for their existence, apart from relatively high bills. It might be worth your while to find alternative heating (even if you can't have the heater removed), but estimate the relative costs first.

Immersion heaters

If your main means of heating water is an immersion heater, use it sparingly. Turn it on and try to do all jobs requiring hot water at one fell swoop. An extra – but maybe tasteless – economy measure is to use "left-over" washing or bathing water to wash floors.

Note that it's cheaper to boil a kettle (even an electric one) than use an immersion heater for small jobs such as washing up.

Alternative heating

If you have no other form of heating, try the measures suggested at the beginning of this section first. Additionally, you can generate warmth in other ways than by crowding a room with people (although this is effective). Turn on the oven or the gas/electricity rings – but low – and stay in their vicinity. Whatever your usual form of heating, it's worth opening the oven after you've cooked something in it: you'd be surprised how much heat remains to be enjoyed!

Paying bills

As mentioned earlier, don't wait to be caught by every enormous quarterly fuel bill. Instead, buy stamps weekly from the appropriate place – gas/electricity showroom or post office – to lessen the burden. Even if you buy more stamps than necessary for the present bill, you've not lost: you can use them for the next quarter's bill. If you're unable to get in to the place(s) every week, put aside a realistic sum for the purpose.

Coping with electricity

Another skill you should suss as soon as you can is coping with electricity. You might think that the wiring where you live is temperamental: this is possible, but it's more likely to be you at fault. Unless the electricity system really is archaic and inefficient, *you* really do have the power to control it (if there is an irredeemable fault in the wiring, you'd better call in an expert).

Speaking as one who's rather afraid of "new-fangled objects" and the electricity they use, I've been amazed at what the stuff can do if you obey its rules:

■ Electricity and water (including heavy condensation) aren't happy bed-fellows. You're liable to eruptions and even personal extinction if you take fires, TVs, etc., into the bathroom. Battery-powered equipment is the exception.

■ If an electrical implement has a 13-amp label, don't dare to fit a 5-amp plug onto it and hope for the best. The best is that you'll wreck a fuse, while there are grades leading up to the worst, which is electrocution: trouble is, you don't know which grade you're going to hit on.

   Generally, all heaters and kettles – anything which warms up quickly, in fact – need the 13-amp treatment. Lamps, razors, record players and so on, should be okay with 5-amp plugs, but do check them before you take that for granted.

■ Ordinary sticky tape isn't terribly efficient as an insulator: using it to join wires, or to hide exposed ones, might give you more than you expected in the way of a buzz. Don't use it!

   If you have noticed bare wires, make sure you turn the power off before you do anything else. Any repairs to damaged wire-casing should then be done *carefully* with insulating tape, which you can buy at hardware stores.

■ Wiring a plug is simple – if you know how. The yellow and green wire is *Earth* (*E*, top centre of a plug). Blue is *Neutral* (denoted by *N* in the plug). Brown is *Live* (denoted, not surprisingly, by *L*). In most plugs there is a fuse. Put the correct fuse in for the equipment you're using. If in doubt, use a 13-amp one which will cope with most things.

More electric points

Other steps you can take, which may not be so obviously life-saving, but do help a lot, include:

■ Reading the instructions on all electrical equipment *before* you plug them in for the first time.

■ Never washing the electrical parts of kettles or any other electric gear.

■ Turning off the electricity at the mains when anyone's fiddling with any implement which is even vaguely connected with/to electricity. I'd advise this even for changing a bulb, after I managed to fuse an entire house when attempting to dislodge a stubborn bulb.

■ Un-plugging all equipment when the house is to be empty for a few days.

■ If everyone's going to be away for more than "a few days", turning off the electricity at the mains.

As you get used to these guidelines, you'll invent or discover more of your own (not the hard way, I hope!). Instead of submitting at the first obstacle – which is almost bound to occur – persevere. Try not to use your "helplessness" as a flirtation point: that might make you an expert at flirtation, but it's not going to help you when you actually *need* to know about electricity.

A final piece of advice: learn to read your meter if you're not paying-as-you-use, after you've determined which implement uses most electricity. Then, you might be able to discover which swines are over-spending, and how you can economise.

Shopping

Shopping is a rotten bind, clever shopping can become an obsessive skill: think about the smug thrill you get when you buy something at one price, and find that a friend has paid ten pence more for exactly the same kind of article at a different place! The difficulty is to ensure that it's always "the other one" who's ripped off. There's no foolproof method, unless you're willing to spend every free moment searching for bargains, but there are some pointers to help you along the right path.

Unfortunately for the individualist, *bulk-buying* is usually the cheapest: if you could share out a whole cow with friends, your own half-pound of minced meat would be cheaper than from a supermarket. Of course, somebody's got to have a freezer for this particular example to be practicable: otherwise, stick to sharing massive packets of soap powder and suchlike. Even if you stock huge amounts of non- or semi-perishable stuff only, even if you only have enough capital to buy slightly-larger-than-minute quantities at one go, it's worth obtaining loads of storage jars.

Storage jars
Don't spend vast amounts of money on fancy storage containers from fancy, expensive shops: there are other ways! Discover a local sweet shop which still sells sweets from jars: the owner/manager might sell the "empties" off cheaply, or even give them away; especially if you're already on friendly terms. These are useful for flour, salt (which you can bulk-buy in health shops where it's purer than the supermarket stuff), rice, biscuits, pasta, oats, muesli etc. – anything, really that keeps well in an airtight jar.

Save or scavenge old ice cream or margarine containers (the big ones) because, without their lids, they're good for organising your fruit and veg, apart from anything else which is inclined to wander if left out. If their dullness offends your sensibilities, you can decorate them; that'll still be cheaper than buying containers from scratch.

Empty coffee, marmalade, jam jars, even yoghurt pots, are useful for dried fruit, lentils, beans and other pulses. Surprisingly enough, some of them look pretty good in the first place; well, they do without their original labels.

For smaller items – I'm really thinking of herbs and spices – you can find quite reasonable-looking containers from branches of "well-known" chemists, where old pill-jars are sold off cheaply. Otherwise, you have to be a mustard freak (or mint saucer, etc.), and wash out the empty jar to find a good container of the right size. When you label the jars – which you should do to avoid confusion – use indelible ink: it's a small point, but enormous frustration has been caused by the handling of such jars with soggy fingers. Would you like a chilli con carne which tastes strongly of cinnamon?

What to store

Once you've accumulated masses of containers, it might be useful
to know what to store in them. It's an idea to make sure that you've
got certain items around all the time, but some of them perish
quickly, so beware. Here's a list of stuff which can be stored
long-term in the "right" conditions:

Inedibles	*Edibles*
Soap powder	Tins (beans, tomatoes, etc.)
Washing-up liquid	Tea
Soap	Coffee
Shampoo	Dried milk
Toothpaste	Flour
Deodorant	*Lard/veg oil
All-purpose cleaner	Dried beans and pulses
Dishcloths	Rice
Soap pads	Pasta
Light bulbs and fuses	Salt
Glue	Pepper
String	Herbs/spices
Sticky tape	Sugar
First-aid gear	Stock cubes

* Fats keep best in a cool place. You can make your own for frying
  by pouring off the remainder from bacon, etc. Store in an airtight
  jar.

Other "regular buys" which might be useful to have around, but
which will only keep for up to a week or so (in good conditions),
include:

Bacon bits	Onions
Bread	Potatoes
Cheese	Spreading marge/butter
Eggs	

How to store

When storing food beware not only of mice, but also of rotting. It's useful to wander round a supermarket and take tips from there: they tend to position their goods to preserve "life" as long as possible. So, going by what the shops do, don't chuck marge or eggs close to radiators; keep them cool at least, if not in a fridge. The exception to this is fruit and veg bought in plastic bags. These need to breathe, and should be "decanted" and stored somewhere cool. Raw meat should only be wrapped loosely, while cooked meat needs cling-filming.

Once tins are opened – as distinct from remaining for years on the shelf – treat the contents as fresh food: any long-life disappears with the vacuum seal.

When to buy food

Knowing how to store and what can be stored becomes valuable information when you realise that one big shopping expedition tends to be relatively cheaper than lots of little piddling ones: you'll spend less if you keep down your trips, because you tend to rely more on a list than lust in that case. The exception to this is in buying addictive luxuries like fags and booze: if you're at all weak-willed and know you've got 200 fags or a crate of beer, you can get through them far too quickly.

Linked with this is the desire to buy more and more unnecessary stuff if you shop when you're hungry; don't. And if you see "pence-off" coupons, use them only if you'd buy the food on offer anyway: do you *really* need half-price hedgehog flavoured crisps? (In case you're wondering, the taste of hedgehog crisps resembles the smell of stale furniture polish).

To help you keep down your shopping expeditions, keep a continuous shopping list of "regular buys" and add items as you're running out of them.

You might have little choice in the matter of when, specifically, to buy. Let's hope you have, because you can really be ripped off if you shop at the "wrong" time of the week, especially for fresh food.

On Saturday mornings, everything's at its most expensive; *late on Saturday afternoons* it's cheapest because shopkeepers want to get rid of stuff which might go bad over the weekend. On Saturday evenings, when the markets are closed, you can even shop for free, if you're neither fussy nor too proud to rustle among rubbish for stuff which has dropped off stalls. In supermarkets, the equivalent bargains are found usually in a place to themselves; they're the ones that have reached their "sell-by" date.

As to availability, Mondays are the worst: so if you're easily tempted to buy extra goodies, Monday might be a good day to shop. *Seasons of availability* don't seem to come into shopping much any more: you can buy virtually anything at all times of the year; strawberries from Israel in December, sprouts from some other distant place in June. But everything is subject to price changes – even spuds may set you back four or five times as much in early summer as in winter.

Here's a general "economy" guide, month by month, but it's not definitive – prices depend on area and harvest, as well as on seasonal changes.

	Vegetables	*Fruit*
All year	Beetroot Cabbage (various) Mushrooms *Onions *Potatoes Radishes Carrots Swedes/turnips Red/green pepper	Apples (different varieties) Bananas Oranges

* Onions and potatoes aren't always cheap, especially in early Summer, but they're true staples for many and are usually less pricey than more exotic vegetables.

	Vegetables	*Fruit*
September	Runner beans Courgettes Marrow	Lemons Melon Pears
October	Aubergine Celery Cucumber Endive Kale Leeks Marrow	English apples Pears
November	Kale Leeks Parsnips Cauliflower	English apples
December	Kale Leeks Parsnips Sprouts Cauliflower	English apples (early December)
January	Kale Leeks Parsnips	
February	Broccoli Sprouts Kale Leeks (which you might be sick of the sight of by now!)	English apples

March	Stick to the reasonable die-hards; no specials this month	
April	Same again – have you tried onion soup?	
May	Cucumber	Rhubarb
June	Cucumber Lettuce	Peaches (As cheap as they'll get)
July	French beans Cucumber Peas New potatoes Avocados	Cherries Gooseberries Lemons Melon
August	Broad beans French beans Cucumber Marrow New potatoes	Lemons Melon Pineapple

Finally, as the price of fruit and veg varies from region to region, so does the price of other foods: you might find something which you thought of as a delicacy to be quite cheap in your new area. If you live near the coast, you could live on fish; if you're in Yorkshire, black pudding and potted meat are a lot cheaper than they'd be in Yeadon.

Where to buy

Apart from knowing the best time of the week and year to buy certain items, it's also worth knowing *where* they're likely to be cheapest. When you first arrive at college, trundle around all your local shops with a list of staples to discover the best bargains: you might get odd stares, but they're nothing to the savings this survey could lead to. Try to have already sussed what you can afford to pay weekly for food: this first "shopping around" will help you to see where your main spending will be; what "necessities" are now going to be luxuries, as well as revealing the bargains. Make sure you compare food weight by weight: packaging can be very deceptive if you only go by size.

To start with, here's a generalised run-down of various kinds of shops and their qualities.

■ *The corner shop* is very convenient and very friendly, yes. It's almost always relatively expensive too, especially if it stays open late and needs to pay staff overtime rates. Unfortunately, you're too poor to lash out on the luxuries of convenience and chattiness: they bite into your grant. The only corner shops whose prices might suit your purse are the ones with an owner-manager, who's slaving away alone to keep the place open for almost twenty-four hours every day.

■ *Supermarkets:* At the beginning of term, when you need soap powder, deodorant, washing-up liquid etc., and can't find a bargain chemist, go to a big supermarket, preferably one which doesn't have deceptively attractive surroundings rather than low prices. You're only in the shop to buy (and maybe to supplement your diet by tasting their free samples); not to admire the decor and be distracted from the job.

As the customer pays in one way or another for the decor of the shop, so he/she also pays for decorative packaging. Generally, the plainer the pack, the cheaper its contents. And you're often onto a winner if the store sells its own brands alongside "well-known" makes: in fact, the goods are sometimes exactly the same, made by the same firm and covered with different wrapping. You might find that the "pretty" one goes to the extent of looking the same size as the plain; its price might even be comparable: check the weight before you buy it.

For general weekly shopping, big supermarkets are often best for tinned and frozen food (and sometimes, for clothes): if there's a delicatessen counter, they might sell you cheese off-cuts or bacon bits quite cheaply too. Otherwise try to avoid their meat or fresh food, which is relatively pricey and sometimes smattered with preservatives to give that "fresh" look. For such stuff, butchers and greengrocers are better; markets are best.

■ *Markets* are the most reliably cheap sources of goods (second only to jumble sales and junk shops). It's not only food they sell cheaply (and cheapest at the end of the day) but everything else, from goldfish to gumboots. Beware, as always, of "prettified" places, which might not be so reasonable; and beware, too, of traders' tricks. When you buy fruit and veg for instance, watch that the stuff you're sold doesn't all come from the back of the stall: it can be very disappointing to find that *your* "beautiful Class 1 Cox" is maggot-ridden; it'll have been waiting at the back specially for a dupe like you.

Get to know the regular traders before you lash out on anything expensive, to be sure that the person who sells you it will still be around next week if you want to return the article or complain.

It's also useful to find out which day is best for what stuff. At my local market, "ordinary" members of the public bring their own old clothes to sell on Tuesdays (now there's an idea for you; if you think you can still make a profit after paying the stall-rent).

Finally, the big difference between markets and shops: haggling. If that's the custom at your local, conform to it – you've only self-consciousness to lose.

■ *Health shops*: When these started out, they tended to be novelties for rich health-freaks. Now, you can find some good bargains in them; especially in the kind which sell from bins and bottles, rather than prepacked. Herbs, pulses, muesli (if you're too lazy to make your own), nuts and dried fruit all tend to be cheaper and purer from health shops. Some also have a good line in information sheets or notice boards, where you can discover the address of your local yoga class, or the date of the next "Vegetarians against the Bomb" meeting.

4. Food and nutrition

Nutrition ■ general hints for healthy eating ■ vegetarianism ■ food allergies ■ three meals? ■ checklist

Nutrition

This is the section I'd have avoided like the plague when I began college: doesn't that heading conjure up pictures of school cookery lessons, or some horrible adult telling you to eat your greens? It certainly does for me!

However, it is important to understand basic nutrition if you're cooking for yourself (or simply eating alone), and also expecting to work and play hard. Malnutrition, which really means poor eating, leads to tiredness and lethargy as well as, eventually, to all sorts of foul internal disorders.

Everyone needs the following essential nutrients in their diet:

Proteins (body-builders): Meat, cheese, nuts, eggs, fish all contain relatively large amounts of first-class protein. Any sort of beans is also protein-rich, but should be backed up with cereals to ensure "glowing" health (actually this is *not* an advert for any well-known breakfast cereals, the ingredients of which tend to contain about as much goodness as their wrapping).

Sugars and Starches (for energy): Cereals, bread, fruit, dried fruit, vegetables are the best sources of natural sugar and starch; a bar of chocolate is not.

Fats (for warmth and long-term energy): Only a small amount is necessary: you'll find plenty in butter, vegetable oils and fats, and nuts.

Vitamins (for "healthy functioning"):
   A – Carrots, tomatoes, dark greens, marge, cheese, eggs.
   B – Cereals, pulses, nuts and yeast extract.

B12 – Meat, fish, eggs, cheese, soya

C – Fruit and greens, especially raw ones.

D – Fish and – sunlight!

E – Leafy vegetables, nuts, eggs, whole cereals, pulses and vegetable oils.

Minerals:

Calcium – Cheese, dried fruit, nuts, whole cereals, beans, dark greens.

Iron – Leafy greens, meat, poultry, eggs, nuts, fruit, shellfish, dried fruit, whole cereals, beans.

Fibre: Whole cereals, fruit and veg.

If this is confusing and/or frightening, don't fret. Indeed, its implications also confuse experts.

You might now think it's not worth bothering about what you eat, and I don't blame you! Perhaps you'll be miserable if you do what "they" say (once you've discovered what the essence of it is): if you don't you *might* have a shorter life, but it could be more fun for food-lovers. Anyway, it's quite easy to get knocked over by buses, isn't it?

Having gone through a phase of the above myself, and also through the other extreme of analysing every edible morsel because "you are what you eat", I suppose I'm a nice, boring moderate in this area now. Even so, I think it's vital to know what is supposed to be healthy and unhealthy, so that you can make up your own mind about how you're going to eat.

As I've said, there are quite a few contradictory ideas flying around about what you need to eat, and in how much quantity. Apart from that, different bodies have different requirements: if you spend twelve hours a day in bed and the rest sitting, you're likely to need fewer calories than a top-class athlete. If you have a speedy metabolism, you burn up food relatively quickly and – you lucky person – you're unlikely to put on fat. To a large extent, you can "feel" what's good for you if you're interested enough to think about it; if not, you can see the results of poor eating in a mirror: spots may be caused by too much grease, overweight can be caused

by eating more than you need. The trick, of course, is to find your
own neat balance: it's probably been fed to you until now by
someone who's learnt from experience; as a student, you've
become your own judge.

General hints for healthy eating

Fortunately for the baffled but willing, most nutritionists do agree
on certain recommendations. One of them is that the British need to
eat more fibre and less fat.

Fat
Fat, particularly animal fat, found in butter and lard, contains
cholesterol, the friend of heart- and arterial-disease. Some cholesterol
is actually necessary: in case you want details, it's produced in the
body when fats are broken down, and is needed to form various
hormones; it's also important in the metabolic process.
Nevertheless, too much is dangerous. To avoid consuming a lot of
cholesterol, keep down your intake of dairy products, including
eggs (okay; not strictly "dairy" stuff): most doctors reckon that
you'd better not eat more than seven eggs a week at the most.

Fibre
From "Eat less fat" there's the transition stage of "What the hell do
we eat?" Well, you now come to the "Fibre brigade". The big
movement away from white flour is heavily supported by fibre
advocates. For those of you who are accustomed to floppy, aerated,
"plastic" bread, the change to brown wholemeal bread might take a
huge effort; but it's worth that. Wholemeal anything – bread,
spaghetti, rice etc. – is more filling and more tasty than its white
counterpart, and it's also healthier. The extra you might pay for
wholemeal should be cancelled out by the fact that you need to eat
less of it.

   White bread, unless artificially "fortified" (which is a bit of a con,
I reckon), has very little fibre compared with wholemeal; so too
have some varieties of brown. If you're going to follow the "fibrous

way", then, make sure you buy genuine wholemeal bread and not the white stuff re-dyed brown, which is often stuffed onto supermarket shelves.

Sugar
Most of you will have had the dangers of sugar shoved into your brains before now. From artificial sweeteners (most of which contain saccharin) to molasses and the purest honey, concentrated sweeteners and sugar are bad for you. Saccharin is an artificial coal-tar derivative, perhaps safer than sugar, but not necessarily harmless. Sugar not only helps to rot your teeth and sprout spots: it's also addictive! If you munch chocolate or sweets regularly, try to replace them with raw fruit and veg. Go easy on sweetened tinned fruit too. Pure fruit and veg contain natural sugar, and are healthier means of getting the necessaries into your body: beware of pure fruit juices however; they, too, have natural sugar but it's so concentrated that there's a bit much for your system to accept happily.

Salt
Until recently, I'd have said that any savoury stuff causes less damage than sweets. Now, research has shown that large amounts of salt are unhealthy too – we can't win, can we? It's the high sodium content that food-specialists are bothered about, which does more damage to some bodies than others, but is generally considered bad for your bones. If you're really keen, you can buy salt with a low sodium content from health shops and chemists. Otherwise, remember that it's better to cook with the stuff and so disperse it, than to ladle it over your prepared food. Similarly, it's healthier not to touch salt-coated savouries. Some of them, like crisps and roasted peanuts, will do you double-mischief in fact – because they're fried!

Artificial additives
What more can I find to seize up your taste buds totally? There's plenty, but I'll stick to one more important hazard, that of artificial

additives. They're found in almost everything, from the juiciest sausages, to the beautifully yellow cheese you've just bought: chances are that the "yellow" comes from a bottle. You'll be hard-pressed then, to cut artificial colour and preservatives altogether, especially as food manufacturers don't have to detail them on packages.

The most commonly decried chemical is *monosodium glutamate*, which is also one of the most commonly used – it'll be in most of those savoury snacks, I'm afraid. Monosodium glutamate is a preservative and flavour-enhancer, and is terribly unhealthy in large quantities.

It's recently been suggested that some additives are not just vaguely harmful, but specifically dangerous to people with certain medical complaints. If you're asthmatic or arthritic, be especially careful to use the purest foods possible: it's not just a case of avoiding the relevant chemicals, because as I've just said, you might not find their details on the food wrappers.

List of ingredients
Lists of ingredients aren't healthy in themselves – in fact it would be interesting to see them in greater detail – but they do offer precautionary tales, if you know how to read into them. Contents have to be listed in order of quantity; the greatest, first. If your tin of soup lists "water" first, it might not seem such a good buy after all.

There are very complicated rules for the titles of goods: a pie filling need not contain much of the meat or fruit you're expecting; "stewing steak" or "tinned pears" contain more. Pure orange juice is the only kind that has to be "pure"; there's "squash" and "drink" too, which include far less orange.

Vegetarianism

According to many people who've written to me about this guide, vegetarianism is the answer to many of the population's dietary problems, whether for economic, environmental or health reasons. There's no doubt that red meat is pricey, and that too much of it is unhealthy (come to think of it, so is too much of anything: did you know that your skin can turn orange if you eat too many oranges?): without any other protein, you can survive on the equivalent of 4 ounces of meat and a pint of milk daily.

The difficulty, when you become vegetarian, is to find the balanced equivalent of this meat; and it is important to find it. Since most of us have been brought up as carnivores, it's easier for us to suss out a balanced meat diet: for vegetarians, cheese butties are not a fair substitute. Nuts, pulses and cereals are all imporant if you cut out meat and fish; so is adventurous cooking if you don't want to be bored into submission.

Veganism, an advanced form of vegetarianism, omits all dairy products, as well as meat, fish and eggs, from the diet. It can be difficult to adopt – and pricey – in certain "backward" areas, and needs a lot of investigation by the individual who's thinking of taking it up. For more information, send a s.a.e. to *The Vegan Society*, 47 Highlands Road, Leatherhead, Surrey.

Food allergies

Now we come to a problem that affects only a minority, but more than you might expect. A food allergy doesn't necessarily mean that you're ill immediately after eating the offending article: it might even mean that you love the food in question, and eat far too much of it. Ironically, there's a close link between addiction and allergy; withdrawal symptoms are one sign of allergy, in fact. Mental as well as physical problems may be caused by a food allergy, but unfortunately, there are still few doctors who recognise this. If you think your lethargy, depression or aggression might be due to a certain food, you'd do well to read *Not all in the mind* by Dr. Richard McKerness (Pan). This explains allergies in detail, as well as suggesting a painful remedy – a five days' fast – and is fascinating to ponder over.

Three meals?

According to nutritionists, it's best to eat "little and often", rather than to starve and stuff: additionally, the smallest meal should be eaten at night when it takes longer to digest. This, for most students, is impractical. It could also be pricey if your only means of having lunch, for example, is buying it in a canteen. You could, of course, take a packed lunch – if you remember to make it! At the other extreme is deciding that you'll skip lunch, and ending up "snacking" on unhealthy junk food because you find yourself starving. Perhaps the most practical thing is to take a load of raw veg around with you during the day, while you make sure you eat a good breakfast and evening meal.

As to the idea that the smallest meal should be the evening one, I'd take it with a pinch of salt (only a pinch!). As long as you eat two hours or more before you go to bed, you should have burnt up enough energy for your stomach to survive: otherwise, your meal will "slouch" through your system and might cause indigestion.

Checklist

To summarise, and to add what I've left out:

■ The best food is usually *raw* food.
■ While cheap cuts of meat should be cooked slowly to tenderise them, veg should be cooked quickly and in the minimum amount of water to retain nutrients.
■ Don't peel veg if possible: their skins contain a lot of goodness. As does the skin of fish.
■ To speed up cooking, and thus save fuel as well as goodness, split the stalks of veg.
■ Pressure cooking is quick and nutrient-saving.
■ Copper pans are neither speedy nor safe; they destroy vitamin C (but those with copper bottoms are okay).
■ Too much fat is bad for hearts, arteries, spots and weight.
■ Too much sugar wrecks teeth as well as other parts of the body. Natural forms of sugar, not concentrated, are the best.

■ Cheese is one of the best "toothpastes" – but it might give you bad dreams because it's difficult to digest.

■ Prunes, rhubarb and pears are efficient, natural laxatives, as is fibrous food, like bran and wholemeal bread.

■ Hard-boiled eggs and bananas "plug up" the system, when you've eaten too many prunes, pears etc.

■ A balanced diet, with moderate amounts of anything, is the most healthy.

Now you've some idea of the healthy way to eat, and how to buy it, you might be interested in some suggestions about how to make it edible!

5. Cookbook

Recipe spiel ■ flavourings ■ cooking tips ■ recipes ■ useful recipe books

After a couple of weeks of marmalade sandwiches and spring rolls, particularly if you're the sort to avoid a *Nutrition* section, you might get *hungry*. This is the time when you're about to splash out on a hunk of meat or – worse – on a real meal in a restaurant. If it gets truly awful and you're too exhausted to use your initiative, hitch home (carefully!). Otherwise, have a go at cooking. The best food is the stuff that you like, the stuff that is cheap and (shame!) the stuff that's good for you.

If you're ready to try your hand at culinary delights, don't stick only to what you know – everything gets boring if you're eating it daily for ten weeks – take risks, and take the rough with the smooth.

Some of you will scorn the idea of cooking to an actual recipe. But – apart from wanting to pad out the book – I do believe that it's useful to have a few tried and tested recipes to hand, to be used and abused.

If you haven't got some of the ingredients (for any recipe; not just mine), most meals will survive with substitutes, or even with a couple of minor omissions. Similarly, accurate measuring is rarely necessary; in fact, you might even prefer to change proportions after trying something if you don't like the taste. So, kitchen scales aren't essential, nor is a trip to the shops if you fancy cooking something for which you haven't got all the ingredients.

Recipe spiel

There are some truly basic recipes in here, for those who think they can burn a boiled egg: there are moderately easy ones, and there's a list of recommended cookery books for those who want to try something different and perhaps more difficult. Actually, I've got a strong idea that if you like tasty food, nothing will be too complicated to cook once you've had a few successes with the basics, so don't despair if you're at the "burn an egg" stage.

In fact, college is the place where lots of people grow into brilliant cooks, if only because it gives them a good excuse to avoid "real" work for a couple of hours. With a radio, record or tape playing alongside, and perhaps a beer waiting as a reward, cooking for friends can be a cheapish way of retaining (or regaining) sanity after a rotten day. It helps greatly if friends chip in with the cost and the washing up.

Washing up

Washing up is the worst bit, but it's got to be done some time. It's best tackled after a meal, and not before the next one. One reason for this is cleanliness, and tidiness; that's not to be dismissed if you live, work, cook, eat and sleep in one room. Apart from that, it's much more difficult to wash dishes after they've "set" with grease and accumulated a layer of dust. If pans have suffered from sticking or burning, soak them for a few hours in warm, soapy water: other dishes rarely need the same treatment.

Try to keep the sink clear of tea leaves, grease and other gunge: plungers work only up to a point – and further measures to clear blocked drains are pricey. Use tea bags, if you've nowhere to chuck the leaves, scrape plates into a bin and, if you can find one, use a sink-strainer that fits over the plughole. Now, there are even washing-up bowls with drainers at the side to allow water, but no muck, down the sink.

Cheap(ish) fuel

If you live with friends and eat together, you can save a lot of cooking fuel, of course. You can save more by cooking several things in the oven when it's on. If separate items need different temperatures, stick the "cooler" cookers in the bottom of the oven (covered in foil if necessary), and check everything regularly to make sure it's all going smoothly. On the top-stove, you can make economies by boiling peas, for example, over a pan of potatoes: the peas need very little cooking, so can be added towards the end of the spuds' cooking time. If you don't mind a mush, chuck veg together into one pan, taking note of their various cooking times.

When you're really hard-up, and can't afford to cook anything, there are two effective solutions apart from raw food. The first is a slow-cooker, which you won't be able to afford now, but might be worth begging for some time: it uses only the equivalent of a light bulb's power. The other, which uses even less fuel, is a *haybox*! Here, get a load of this – but only for soup, vegetable and bean stews, etc., not for meat or fish.

Stuff a cardboard box (about 24" × 15") with old clothes (clean ones!) moulded round a saucepan. Bring the pan of food to the boil on the top of a stove and keep it bubbling for a couple of minutes. Then, *run like fury* to the haybox – simultaneously wiping the pan-base to get rid of stray sparks. Put the lid on the pan, chuck some more clothes over it and around, and cover the lot with a tray until you want to serve the meal. Cooking times are as follows:

  Potatoes: two hours
  Porridge: overnight
  Beans: all day
  Stews: all day

In case you're wondering, this is not an April Fool's joke, or any other: my mother often used this method of cooking when she was skint, and she thinks it works!

Flavourings

Flavourings (and I'm *not* talking about the chemical productions) are virtually indispensable to poverty-stricken students. And tomato ketchup is all very well at first, but not for ever. You can buy herbs and spices most cheaply in bulk from health shops, or from chemists: the purist will retort that they "go off"; but for most people, dried herbs keep adequately for ages in an airtight jar. Otherwise, grow your own; it's not difficult. Chives and parsley do taste much better fresh, and they're easy to grow on a window sill.

If you're not really interested, but fancy a bit of flavour, chuck a few mixed herbs in with your special dishes: for those who'd like to get "seriously" into flavourings, here's a list to help you start:

- ■ *Basil*: has a sweetish smell. It goes well with virtually anything, especially with Italian dishes and tomatoes. Try it also with peppers, aubergines, fish, meat (when it's better partnered with garlic), chicken, eggs, sausagemeat and shellfish. It has a very special flavour, so be careful which other herbs you mix it with.
- ■ *Bay*: Best as whole leaves, which are removed after cooking, bay goes with most things too, particularly tomatoes and onions.
- ■ *Bouquet garni*: comes in sachets which bear a remarkable resemblance to tea bags: it's a mixture of herbs. Again, remove the sachet before serving the grub.
- ■ *Caraway*: usually comes in seed form. It has a very distinctive taste, so don't use it on friends until you know they like it. Caraway goes with cabbage, pork and goulash.
- ■ *Cardamon*: need only bother you if you're into making real curries, of which it's a main ingredient.
- ■ *Chilli*: is – guess what? – the basis of chilli con carne. It's a hot pepper which also brightens up bland food, like that tin of baked beans.
- ■ *Chives*: While most herbs are bought ready-dried and are added during cooking, chives are best fresh and added when the food is almost or already cooked. They're also stylish over raw food like cucumber or yoghurt. Chives have an oniony flavour, which isn't surprising, because they're a kind of onion.
- ■ *Cinnamon*: Cinnamon is usually used in sweet dishes. For a rather select experience, mix it with sugar, and sprinkle on buttered toast.
- ■ *Cloves*: These can be overpowering if you're not careful. You've probably heard of them in apple pies, but they're also good in beef stews and "proper" curries.
- ■ *Coriander*: It's quite easy to remember which spices go into real curries, because most of them begin with "C". Here's another which, according to those who know about such things, smells like bed-bugs. It can also be used in sweet dishes; some cake recipes contain coriander.

- *Cumin*: Yes another curry flavouring. In fact, it's good in any spicy dishes, and is often used in chilli con carne. Apparently it was once considered an aid to the pale, interesting look – I've never tried it for that. It has a powerful flavour, so use it sparingly.

- *Curry powder*: This is *not* the sole ingredient of real curry – although Indians do use an equivalent called *Garam masala* as a basis for some of theirs. If you're not a curry expert, this powder's fair enough: it comes in various strengths.

- *Dill*: You'll be lucky to find dill in the shops, but it's worth the search. Dill weed is one of the main ingredients used in pickling cucumbers; it also goes well with courgettes and cheese. Dill seed is good sprinkled over salad, and particularly yoghurt and cucumber salad.

- *Garlic*: A love/hate herb. Best bought fresh in bulbs from the greengrocer, you prize off a clove, peel it and chop the inside very finely. Though it doesn't taste especially strong when you eat it, others will notice you've had it: as you sweat, its aroma oozes through your pores.

  In spite of that, I'd rather use it than not. You can rub it over meat, stick it in anything containing minced meat, make salad dressing with it; you can even rub it around the bowl into which you're going to put a salad.

  It's also got healing properties (I am not an old wife; I don't tell tales): it helps to cure colds and is good for your voice; but that might be because you *have* to project when garlic–haters move to the other end of a room.

- *Geranium*: I used to think it was only a pretty flower, too. Apparently, the leaves are very good in sweet dishes of fruit or jelly.

- *Ginger*: This comes in many forms: fresh ginger is milder than powdered. It can be ground to a pulp and put in curries. Ground, it gives a kick to anything sweet. Crystallised ginger is an expensive sweet, eaten on its own and very strong!

- *Horseradish*: This, basically, isn't a herb, but it can be used with grated apple as a garnish for fish, added to salad cream to go with chicken and egg salads, as well as in horseradish sauce to ladle over your roast beef! Well, you can always hope!

■ *Ketchup*: Tomato ketchup, for most things, is an expensive way of removing the true taste of your food, as opposed to adding to it.

Mushroom ketchup, however, can be used sparingly (has to be used sparingly; it's very strong) in much the same way as Worcester sauce, to perk up anything which is otherwise boring.

■ *Mace*: Mace comes from nutmeg: it's pricier, but that needn't bother you too much because it's used in such small amounts. A bit more delicate than nutmeg, it's used in soups, stews and cakes as well as curries.

■ *Marigold*: Marigold petals are the poor person's saffron: they do the same colouring job, as well as adding a slight bitterness. You can plonk the leaves in food too, but those are quite coarse as well as bitter.

■ *Marjoram*: Marjoram is a milder version of thyme. Use it in stuffing; with veg such as aubergines, courgettes, peppers and tomatoes; in meat sauces, fish and soup.

■ *Mint*: Best fresh, sprinkled on lamb and veg, especially potatoes and peas. You can also put it in fruit salad.

■ *Nasturtium*: You can use the leaves in salads or sandwiches, but the best delicacy is from the seeds and takes time: wash them, and leave in a bottle of salted vinegar for a few days; you then have a cheap substitute for capers. The flavoured vinegar is tasty, too.

■ *Nutmeg*: This is usually used in sweet dishes, but you can also chuck grated nutmeg into sausage casseroles, over spinach and cheese. It also makes alcoholic drinks far more potent but too much is poisonous, so be careful!

■ *Oregano*: Oregano is also called "wild marjoram", just to confuse you; as you might expect, it's stronger than its cousin. Use it for anything vaguely Italian – pizzas, spaghetti bolognese, lasagne, etc. – as well as chilli con carne. Ratatouille also gets a kick from oregano; so does any food which could do with strong flavouring.

- *Parsley*: Best fresh, and easy to grow. You can use it in cooking, or just sprinkled over food or sauces.
- *Pepper*: For most purposes, freshly ground black pepper is the best. *Cayenne* is very strong pepper; similar in flavour to chilli powder, but finer. *Paprika* should be bright red; it's very mild and can be sloshed over food without endangering delicate throats. Use it in goulashes.
- *Rosemary*: Rosemary has a very distinctive, bitterish taste, which some people find offensive. If you don't, you'll like it with meat, especially lamb.
- *Saffron*: Saffron is the most expensive spice in the world, costing more – ounce for ounce – than gold (or so rumour has it): fortunately, it's very light. You're unlikely to need it unless you're a gourmet cook, but it is good for colouring (yellow) as well as flavouring, and is used most commonly in paella, cakes and hot cross buns!
- *Sage*: Sage is much more than just half of sage-and-onion stuffing: it goes with sausages and any other meat which needs strong flavouring, and with liver.
- *Savory*: Savory is a stronger version of thyme. Use it with sausagemeat, and with peas and beans.
- *Sorrel*: Sorrel is rather spinach-like and is most often used in fish recipes.
- *Tabasco*: You'll find this most often as a very hot sauce – it's a useful standby to chuck in bland food towards the end of cooking.
- *Tarragon*: Tarragon vinegar is very delicate, and is only used in "posh" dishes generally: the herb, too, is quite delicate, so I wouldn't bother to have it as a basic. When you become expert, though, try it.
- *Thyme*: This *is* one of the basics: use it in everything, especially when combined with onion and garlic. Any of the tomato, pepper, courgette-type vegetables are also tastier for a touch of thyme, which is a bit milder than the other all-purpose herb, sage.
- *Turmeric*: Like saffron, turmeric colours food yellow; but it

should be used as a substitute for saffron, or vice versa. Turmeric can be used in curries or sweet dishes; its flavour isn't particularly strong.

Cooking tips

Hoping that the above might have instilled in you a yearning for something more adventurous than beans on toast I've compiled a list to help the "novice" get into reasonable habits: it's not definitive; if you discover more, pass them on to friends.

- *Apples*: Dunking chopped apples – and bananas or pears for that matter – in lemon juice for a minute, stops them browning and adds a tang.
- *Booze*: Adding booze to cooking, gives it style, but some recipes ask for stuff you can't afford to drink straight, let alone chuck in cooking. Remember that once booze is boiled, it loses its alcoholic content, so add it as you're serving if you want to retain the full effect: recipes which ask for cooking with alcohol are best taken word for word; often the booze is used as a flavouring, and not intended to make you tipsy. If you're skint, substitute:
  a) cider for wine.
  b) wine vinegar for dry wine – but only use a drop, because it'll blow your head off otherwise.
  c) sherry, sweet wine or fruit juice for spirits.
  If you do use wine in cooking, get the cheapest, plonkiest: a recipe will benefit more from it than your stomach when it's "neat".
- *Bread*: Don't chuck away stale bread. As long as it's not green at the edges (by which time it's too late for any revival), you can wrap it in a damp cloth for a few moments, then warm it (*after* you've removed the cloth!) for a short time in a hot oven. Comes up a treat, just like the baker meant it to be. Otherwise, you could slice or dice it and then harden it in the oven. Stored in an airtight container, the bread can be kept to chuck in soup, or to be grated and used as breadcrumbs.

- *Breakfast cereals*: If you must buy them, buy the biggest pack possible and close properly after each meal. Add your own sugar, or do without, instead of spending more on the ones that are already coated. Similarly, avoid ready-made mueslis which contain up to 25% sugar content: it's cheaper and easy to make your own.

- *Cheese*: Vacuum-packed cheese tends to be blander and more expensive than chunks from a block. Cheapest are cheese-ends or grated cheese. Store it in greaseproof paper in a cool place; in an airtight container too, if there's a risk of mice.

- *Cream*: Top of the milk makes fine cream when beaten. If you're splashing out, use real cream mixed with 1 beaten egg-white per 5-ounce carton, to make it go further.

- *Eggs*: Put them in room-heat for about half-an-hour before using to get their full flavour. Otherwise, keep them in a cool place. Test for freshness by sitting them in water: bad ones float.

- *Lemon juice*: Adds a tang to many foods, as well as preventing certain fruits from browning (see *Apples*). It's cheaper to buy in bottles than to squeeze your own.

- *Marge wrappers*: or the dregs from plastic containers can be saved to grease baking tins.

- *Meat*: Cover raw meat loosely with paper to let it breathe; and with plastic film if cooked. This stops it drying out, and prevents flies from getting at it before you.

- *Melon*: Test a melon for ripeness by pressing your thumbs into the non-stalk end: if softish, it's almost ready; if very soft, it's over-ripe and you might be able to afford it after haggling with the greengrocer.

- *Milk*: Dried milk is adequate for most purposes, and is usually low-fat. If you do prefer the real stuff, buy it in bottles which are cheaper than cartons. Keep milk cool in a basin of water, if you've no access to a fridge.

- *Old fruit*: Cut out the bad bits and then stew it, if stewable, in a little water or milk.

- *Old veg*: Use any old veg, raw or cooked for soup. Chuck in a stock cube and seasoning to add flavour.

- *Packets*: Open them out when they're finished; you'll be surprised at how much contents still lurks.
- *Potatoes*: Stop cut ones browning by putting them in water.
- *Ready-mixes*: They have a tendency to taste like their outer wrappers. If you must use them, add your own flavourings to make them resemble real food.
- *Rhubarb*: Don't eat the leaves; they're poisonous. The redder the stalk, the sweeter the flavour.
- *Rice*: Buy the cheapest, plainest variety: if you prefer it tarted up, do it yourself with herbs and/or veg.
- *Tins*: Instead of buying tin after tin of dried milk, coffee etc., use the first empty one as a container for packet re-fills, which are cheaper.
- *Tinned fruit*: Unless stewed in its own juice without sugar, tinned fruit isn't good for you: unadulterated, the juice sieved from tins makes a drink for non-alcoholics.
- *Tinned veg*: If you must buy them, the chopped varieties are usually the best value.
- *Tomatoes*: Cheap, squashy ones are often tastier for cooking than the tinned variety – but only buy them if they're not actually rotting. You can peel any tomato without hassle by scoring it round the middle and dumping it for a minute or two in very hot water.
- *Yoghurt*: You can use yoghurt for almost any recipe which asks for cream. Make it yourself by saving some (about a dessertspoonful per pint) from the last lot, mixing it with hand-hot milk and leaving it in a closed, wide-necked vacuum flask for about eight hours. Make thick, low-fat yoghurt by using more dried milk to water than the instructions state.

Cooking times

As I've mentioned, it's quicker and more nutritious to chop veg up small, chuck them into boiling, salted water and cook them swiftly.

The same can't be said for meat: the cheaper the cut, the longer and slower the cooking time for edible results. Here's a list of averages, but add about five minutes per pound for really grotty stuff:

Beef:	20 mins. per lb. + 20 mins.	Gas 5
Chicken:	20 mins. per lb. + 15 mins.	Gas 5
Fish:	5–10 mins. each side	Grill/fry
Lamb:	25 mins. per lb. + 20 mins.	Gas 5
Pork:	30 mins. per lb. + 20 mins.	Gas 5
Rabbit:	about an hour for an average one	Gas 3

It's better to overcook chicken and pork if you don't want salmonella poisoning, than to undercook it. The meat should be tender when you stick a knife in, with no blood traces left.

Oven temperatures

Okay, none of the above makes sense because you have one of those ovens which goes from "cool" to "very hot". Here you go, then:

Very low/cool	Gas $\frac{1}{4}-\frac{1}{2}$	240–250F	100–140C	(approx.)
Low/slow	Gas 1–3	275–325F	150–170C	(approx.)
Moderate/warm	Gas 4–5	350–375F	180–190C	(approx.)
Hot	Gas 6–7	400–425F	200C	(approx.)
Very hot	Gas 8–10	450–500F	210–250C	(approx.)

Weights and measures

The recipes I've given have imperial weights and measures, where any. To be realistic, I reckon you might need a sensible conversion, into items like spoons and mugs: every spoon measure I've given is rounded – which means there should be as much stacked on top of the spoon as there is in the bowl, but not more (the exception, you'll be glad to know, is the liquid measurement).

■ A cup is about an inch below the top of a half-pint mug.
■ A small cup is about half that.
■ If you can't find a half-pint mug or milk bottle, use the following:
  – $\frac{1}{4}$ pint of liquid is equal to 6 tablespoons
  – $\frac{1}{4}$ lb. flour (1 cup) equals 6 tablespoons
  – $\frac{1}{4}$ lb. sugar (1 small cup) equals 4 tablespoons
  Not a tablespoon in the house?
  – 2 dessertspoons equal 1 tablespoon
  – 2 teaspoons equal 1 dessertspoon

Recipes

Here's what a lot of all that spiel was leading up to: recipe time. To be honest, not all of these are my own: thanks to the imagination of some *Guardian* readers, several friends and present students, there's more variety than I could have dreamt up.

Soups

Soup is a cheap, nourishing filler, either before a meal or as one. Some people hate it; but the actual taste is often far more exciting than the idea of it. If you really feel repulsed by the thought of eating the stuff, it might be because you were brought up on the cardboard kind from packets, or the sugary squelch in cans (although some aren't quite as awful as that).

Even if you've adored soup from an early age, it's advisable to avoid certain packets – especially the "cup" breed – which are mostly chemical conglomerates rivalling only papier maché in the taste stakes: that's my opinion, anyway.

Better than any pre-packed gunge, and sometimes little more bother than opening them, is your own make. Apart from giving you the smug satisfaction of knowing it's "home-made", your concoctions will often taste better and be healthier for you. Once you've got the gist of basic soup-making, you can chuck virtually anything in them, including most left-overs and the outer leaves of veg or lettuce which you'd rather not eat "pure". The green-grocer might even be chatted up to give you things like turnip-tops or cauliflower casings, which can't be sold in any case: they can all be put in soup.

Be careful, though with meat left-overs: put them in just before serving so that they heat through but don't re-cook; food-poisoning is rather a dubious way of avoiding unwelcome lectures. You should be okay with most meat, but pork and chicken are a bit dodgy, and the risk isn't really worth taking.

The one disadvantage of poverty as a soup-maker is your likely lack of a liquidiser or blender: either is excellent for thick, smooth soups. But don't let that put you off totally; you can sieve the soup if you're that bothered, or chop up the veg so small that they almost mash themselves.

There are dozens of soup recipes; basically, you're just boiling veg in less water than usual, and retaining the flavoured water to drink with the resultant mush. *Don't* take any of these recipes as gospel: as I've said, anything can be soupified, and few of the veg I mention are sacred to the recipe. Do go easy on carrots and celery if you don't want them to overwhelm other ingredients; both are rather strong.

If you're eating alone and can't be bothered to make minute quantities, cover what you don't use and keep it cool – it should be fine for a day or two.

■ *Basic (thin) soup*

2 stock cubes
1 pt. water
1 oz. fat
1 small carrot
1 small parsnip
1 small onion/leek
1/2 celery stalks
salt and other seasoning

Preparation and cooking: about 30 mins.
Serves: 2/3

Clean the veg by washing, scraping and peeling if necessary. Cut them all up, into long strips, dice or whatever you fancy. Boil the water and dissolve the stock cubes in it, then put in a pan. Add the fat and a small pinch of salt (stock cubes already contain some salt).

Chuck in the veg and boil up. Cover the pan, and simmer slowly for about 20 minutes, or until everything is soft. And that is that!

■ *Basic (thick) soup*

As above, but add 1 oz. flour to the fat.

Also, replace some of the water with milk if you like.

Preparation and cooking: about 30 mins.
Serves: 2/3

As with most sauces, you only have to add flour to make it thick, but you've got to do it carefully: flour has an awkward habit of going lumpy if you forget about stirring it.

Before you put anything else in the pan for thick soup, melt the fat and stir in the flour over a low heat. Let it cook slowly for a couple of minutes.
Add the liquid gradually, stirring all the time. Sieve the mixture if it still goes lumpy.
Add more seasoning than with the thin soup, because flour tends to neutralise flavours. Pepper's a good idea; so are any herbs you've got.

■ *Basic lentil soup*

Small tin tomatoes
Water
Onion

Carrots
2 oz. red lentils
stock cube

Preparation and cooking: about 40 mins.
Serves: 1

Seasoning (including soy sauce, if possible)
Open the tomatoes and put them in the pan. Fill the can with water and add that.
Peel onion, scrape the carrots and chop both. Chuck them into the pan, together with the lentils and a stock cube and/or soy sauce.
Boil it all up, making sure that the stock cube dissolves. Lower the heat, cover the pan and cook gently for about 30 minutes.
You can add grated or cottage cheese for taste, and eat with wholemeal bread if you want to make a full meal of it.

■ *Potato and leek soup* (simple)

1 leek
8 oz. potato
$\frac{1}{2}$ pt. water
salt and pepper
herbs if you like

Preparation and cooking: about 20 mins.
Serves: 1

Chop up the leek and potato, chuck into a pan with the water and seasoning, and boil until it's soft. Mash the soup if you like.

■ *Carrot and leek soup*

8 oz. leeks	Worcester sauce
8 oz. carrots	salt and pepper
small clove garlic	2 tsp. fat
1 pt. (or a bit more) water	
2 stock cubes – pref. chicken or \veg.	

Preparation and cooking: about 30 mins.
Serves: 2

Trim the leeks, leaving as much green as you think edible, and halve lengthwise. Chop and wash. Scrape the carrots and chop into small chunks. Peel and chop onion.
Heat the fat and add veg.
Chop the garlic and add that. Stir to coat it all in fat.
Cover the pan and cook gently for about 10 minutes.
Add boiling water and the stock cubes, plus salt and pepper.
Simmer the lot for 10 minutes.
If you're feeling diligent or rich, sieve or liquidise everything (warm the liquidiser first, to avoid shattered glass).
Put everything back into the pan, add a few drops of Worcester sauce and keep hot until you want to eat.

■ *"Cream" of celery soup*

1 pt. water
$1\frac{1}{2}$ chicken/veg stock cubes
1 small head celery (top-leaves too)
$\frac{1}{2}$ tsp. salt or celery salt
1 oz. fat
1 oz. flour
$\frac{1}{2}$ tsp. yeast extract
1 small onion

Preparation and cooking: about 40 mins.
Serves: 2/3

Wash the celery and slice. Peel and chop the onion.
Melt half the fat in a pan, add celery and stew gently for about five minutes, stirring occasionally to prevent sticking. Meanwhile, boil the water and dissolve the stock cube in it. Then add most of the stock and cook until the celery's tender (about 10–20 minutes, depending on how small you've chopped the celery).
Either transfer the celery to a plate, or melt the rest of the fat in another pan (if you're flush with pans), and cook the onions gently for about five minutes.
Sprinkle the flour over the onions and cook for a couple of minutes.
Add the celery and all the stock. Cook for about 15 minutes, stirring whenever you remember to.
Add the yeast extract, the salt and chopped celery leaves.
Cook gently for at least another five minutes, with the lid on if you don't want ot lose liquid.

■ *Flemish soup*
(thick, "superior" veg)

12 oz. potatoes
12 oz. carrots
1 large onion
1 small leek
few sticks of celery
1 oz. fat
$\frac{1}{2}$ tsp. yeast extract
1 pt. water
1 stock cube
2 tsps. top-of-the-milk (if poss.)
pinch marjoram
salt and pepper

Preparation and cooking: about 1 hour.
Serves: 2/3

Wash and chop all the veg (peeling the onion, first).
Melt half the fat, add the carrots and cook very gently.
In order, gradually add celery, potatoes, leeks and onions.
Cook the lot gently for about 10 minutes, stirring occasionally.
Boil the water, dissolve the stock cube in it and add about half to the cooking veg.
Simmer until all the veg are soft.
Now's the time to sieve everything if you're going to.
Once that's done (or not, as the case may be), chuck everything back in the pan, add the rest of the stock and bring to the boil. Add the rest of the fat, the yeast extract, the marjoram, salt and pepper; and simmer for about 20 minutes.
If you're using top-of-the-milk, tip it in just before serving.
Swirl it into the serving dishes, and it looks very stylish!

■ *Frankfurter soup*

This sort of soup is worth coming home to when you're cold, wet and/or dejected. With some bread, it's probably enough for a main course.

1 pt. water	2 onions or leeks
1½ beef stock cubes	2 oz. bacon bits (when trimmed of fat)
1 medium potato	
turnips/swedes/carrot/celery/ about 8 ozs.	3 frankfurters

Preparation and cooking: about 1½ hours.
Serves: 2/3

Boil the water and dice the potatoes at the same time.
Add the stock cubes to the water, and the potatoes and chuck them in a pan.
Simmer for about 10 minutes until the potatoes are soft but not too mushy.
Meanwhile, wash and chop the veg up small.
Cut up the bacon and cook it alone in its own fat.
Remove the spuds from the pan when they're soft (using a serrated spoon if you've got one) and bash them with a fork to make a mush.
Put everything, except the frankfurters into the pan and bring to the boil. Then lower the heat, cover the pan and cook gently for about 1 hour to blend the flavours.
When you're about ready to eat, slice the frankfurters, chuck them in the pan and warm them through. The soup is now ready.

■ *French onion soup*
(for beginners)

1 tbsp. marge/butter	scant 2 pts. water
1 tbsp. oil	2 beef stock cubes
smattering of sugar	3 slices of bread (1 per person)
12 oz. onions	4 oz. grated cheese
1 clove garlic	mustard

Preparation and cooking: 1½ hours.
Serves: 2/3

Peel and slice the onions. Melt the butter and oil, and gently fry onions, sugar and garlic for about half-an-hour, not allowing the onions to blacken. There should be a thin brown film of sugar on the bottom of the pan when you've done.

While the onions are cooking, boil the water and dissolve your stock cubes in it.

Once the onions are ready, pour in the stock and simmer gently for an hour, with the pan lid on. Add salt and pepper afterwards.

Toast the bread on one side under a grill, turn it over and spread the mustard and cheese on the uncooked side. Melt the cheese until it's glue-like in texture, but not browned.

Put it in the bottom of the soup bowl – chopped up if necessary or preferred – and pour the soup over. This soup, served with salad, is a main course.

■ *Potato soup with bacon bits*

8 oz. potatoes	1 pt. water
1 large carrot	1 stock cube
1 stick of celery	1 pinch marjoram
1 small swede/turnip (or bits of)	handful bacon bits
1 small onion	salt and pepper
1 oz. fat	

Preparation and cooking: about 1 hour.
Serves: 2

Wash and chop the potatoes, swede/turnip and onion (peeling the onion and swede first). Scrape the other veg and chop them, too (and put the swede and potato in water if you don't want them to brown).

Melt the fat, add the veg and stir to coat.

Cover the pan and let the lot simmer for about 10 minutes.

Next, pour in the stock and add the marjoram, salt, pepper and water (if the stock's not already dissolved in it).

Put the lid partly on, leaving an air-vent, and simmer for about 20 minutes.

The conscientious now do their sieving, and return the mixture to the pan.

Meanwhile, grill the bacon. Add that to the soup and eat.

■ *Health soup*

2 oz. ready mix	8 oz. chopped veg of your choice
barley/corn/beans (not the kind	salt
that should be soaked for	dill
hours)/oatmeal, etc.	1/2 tbsp. yoghurt
$\frac{3}{4}$ pint water	

Preparation and cooking: about 1 hour.
Serves: 1/2

Put the water, ready-mix and salt in the pan and boil them up. Cook for about 10 minutes and then add the veg. Continue cooking until the veg are soft. Add the dill and cook for about 10 minutes' more. Just before serving, add the yoghurt.

■ *Red lentil soup*

4 oz. red lentils	1 vegetable stock cube
1 carrot	1 oz. fat
1 small leek	1 heaped tbsp. flour
1 onion	1 bayleaf
4 oz. potatoes	salt
1 pint water	herbs as they appeal to you

Preparation and cooking: about $1\frac{1}{2}$ hours.
Serves: 2/3

Cook the lentils in half the water for about 30 minutes, till they're soft. Meanwhile, peel the onion, scrape the carrot and wash the onion and potatoes. Chop them all up quite small.

Melt half the fat in a pan, add the onions and potatoes, and stew gently for about five minutes, stirring occasionally to prevent sticking.

Boil the water that remains and add the stock cube, then pour into the onion/potato mix. Cook until the veg are soft.

Melt the rest of the fat in a separate pan, add the flour and leave them alone for a couple of minutes over a low heat. Gradually add the other stuff, stirring all the time to fight off lumps, and boil for five minutes; then add the bayleaf salt and any other seasoning.

Simmer everything for about half an hour before eating it.

■ *Soya bean soup*

1 tbsp. oil
2 tbsp. soya flour
$\frac{3}{4}$ pt. water
1 beef stock cube
1 small tsp. yeast extract
1 small onion
1 tomato
pepper

Preparation and cooking: about $1\frac{1}{2}$ hours.
Serves: 2/3

Peel and chop the onion, and skin the tomato if it's not from a tin.

Melt the oil and fry the veg gently for about 10 minutes, until they're soft.

Stir in the soya flour and cook for a couple of minutes.

Having made stock with boiled water and the stock cube, add it gradually to the mixture, stirring to prevent lumpiness.

Bring this lot to the boil, add the yeast extract and simmer for about fifteen minutes.

Add pepper, plus any herbs you fancy; you're unlikely to need salt because of what's already in the yeast extract and stock cube.

■ *Tomato soup*

This recipe makes tasty soup. If you replace the milk with extra water, it's also pretty good as a sauce for spaghetti or other dishes.

1 15 oz. tin of tomatoes
1 onion
1 oz. fat
1 oz. flour
2 tsps. lemon juice
pinch of sugar (optional)
$\frac{1}{2}$ pt. water
1 beef stock cube
$\frac{1}{2}$ pt. milk
1 bay leaf
garlic (optional)
mixed herbs
salt and pepper

Preparation and cooking: about 25 mins.
Serves: 2/3

Open the tin of tomatoes and chop up the contents. Peel the onions and chop them finely.
Melt half the fat in a saucepan and fry the onions gently; then add the tomatoes and the flour, and stew it for a couple of minutes.
Meanwhile, boil the water, add the stock cube and dissolve it: then add that to the saucepan mixture, stirring to avoid lumps.
Next add the bay leaf, lemon juice, salt and pepper and herbs, the sugar and garlic too, if you're using them at all.
Simmer it all for ten minutes, stirring when you remember to.
This tastes best with grated cheese, if you've any handy.

■ *Vegetable semolina soup*

1 tbsp. semolina
1 pt. water
1 stock cube
$\frac{1}{2}$ small onion
$\frac{1}{2}$ leek
2 small carrots
1 small turnip
bit of cauliflower
scant 1 oz. fat
1 tsp. yeast extract
1 bay leaf
salt
fresh parsley, if possible

Preparation and cooking: about 1 hour.
Serves: 2/3

Clean the veg peel if necessary and cut into small cubes or strips; that's your choice.
Melt most of the fat in a pan and stew the veg in it for about 10 minutes, stirring when you remember.
Add the boiled water and stock cube, and cook till everything's tender. Then add the bay leaf.
Pour in the semolina, stirring slowly – otherwise it may go lumpy.
Cook gently for about 30 minutes, then add the yeast extract and the last drop of fat.
Salt it to taste before serving, and sprinkle parsley on top if you have any.

Snacks, main dishes and accompaniments

The following recipes are put down in an unprofessional but, I hope, simple order. They're in alphabetical order, going by the first initial of the main ingredient. The exception is SALAD, with a section of its own under "S".

Have a go – good luck!

Bacon

■ *Left-over burgers*

2/3 rashers bacon or bits
cold, cooked meat
small onion
a few mushrooms

3 oz. breadcrumbs (3 average slices of bread, grated)
mixed herbs
packet of crisps (if you're not worried about nutrition)

Preparation and cooking: about 15 mins.
Serves: 2

Remove any rind from the bacon and chop it up. Cook it in its own fat.
Chop the other ingredients up.
Remove the bacon and mix it with everything else except the crisps.
Form the mixture into flat cakes, coat with crisps and grill or fry.
If you like, serve the burgers in bread rolls.

■ *Bacon casserole*

8 oz. bacon (after it's been
de-rinded and de-fatted)
2 medium onions
2 large potatoes
chicken stock cube
$\frac{1}{4}$—$\frac{1}{3}$ pt. water
salt and pepper

Preparation and cooking: about 2 hours.
Serves: 2/3

Chop the bacon finely, and put half of it at the bottom of a greased dish.

Chop the onions, put half of them in a layer over the bacon.

Peel and thinly slice the potatoes, and put half of them in a layer over the onions.

Repeat the layers.

Boil the water, add the stock cube and seasoning, and tip it over the other ingredients.

Shove everything into an oven on Gas 3 (325F or about 150C) for $1\frac{1}{2}$ hours.

Serve the casserole with vegetables and/or bread.

It can be re-heated at a low temperature for 20–25 minutes.

For a richer meal, replace the stock with a white sauce.

Melt 1 oz. fat, add 1 oz. flour and allow it to cook for a few minutes.

Then add $\frac{1}{2}$–$\frac{3}{4}$ pt. milk or milk and water, gradually.

Slowly bring the sauce to the boil, stirring all the time and season.

Then tip this over the bacon, onion and potato.

Cabbage

■ *Bigos*

cabbage/sauerkraut
any left-over meat
salt and pepper

Preparation and cooking: 10 mins–1 hour.
Serves: as many as you like

Cook the cabbage or sauerkraut, add the meat and heat through. If you're hungry, it takes about 10 minutes. If you can wait for the flavours to mingle, allow 1 hour or more for it to cook over a slow heat.

This is a Polish dish suggested by a Guardian reader, who says that Polish peasants call it "the everlasting meal". They keep a pan of cabbage always at the ready, and add left-over meat as it turns up.

■ *Bubble and squeak*

onion, 1 medium between 2   tomato purée
left-over cabbage   oil
left-over potatoes   salt and pepper

Preparation and cooking: 15 mins.
Serves: as many as you like

This is another left-over meal, really, but it's tasty enough to start
from scratch, in which case add about 15 minutes to the preparation
time, to peel and cook the potatoes and cabbage.
If they're not already done, peel the potatoes and mash them.
Chop the onion and fry it gently in oil.
Remove the onion, leaving the fat.
Mix together equal amounts of finely chopped cabbage and mash,
add onion, salt and pepper and a teaspoon per person of tomato
purée or ketchup.
Re-heat the oil and spoon in the mixture so that it's a pancake about
an inch thick.
Fry on both sides until golden and serve.

■ *Chick pea cook-up*

small tin of chick peas   1 tbsp. fat (preferably oil)
(or about 8 oz. when cooked)   1 tsp. oregano
4 oz. cabbage   salt and pepper
2 tomatoes
1 stick celery

Preparation and cooking: about 30 mins.
Serves: 2

Chop the celery and cabbage quite finely. Heat the fat and fry the
above until they're squodgy.
Chop the tomatoes and drain the chick peas, then add them to the
mixture, with all the other ingredients.
Shove a lid on the pan and cook gently for about 20 mins.

Cheese

■ *Cheese on toast*

2 slices bread   2/3 oz. cheese

Preparation and cooking: about 10 mins.
Serves: 1

Grill 1 side of the bread, turn over and place slices of hard cheese on top. Grill until melted and browning.

There's only one problem I can envisage with this recipe – even if you can burn a boiled egg – and that is not having a grill. If all is well, however, and you fancy getting adventurous, try variations:

■ *Cheese and egg on toast*

2 slices bread   1 egg
1/2 oz. cheese

Preparation and cooking: about 10 mins.
Serves: 1

Exactly the same as above, except that you should grate the cheese and mix it with the egg before spreading it on the bread.

■ *Cheese, bacon and chutney toast*

1 dessertsp. chutney   1 oz. grated cheese
1 dessertsp. milk   1/2 rashers bacon
1 slice bread

Preparation and cooking: about 12 mins.
Serves: 1

Toast the bread on both sides. Mash the grated cheese with milk, spread the chutney on the toast and add the cheese mixture.
Grill the bacon and add the toast, at its side, to brown.
Once you've mastered the basic cheese on toast to your liking, try adding new flavours, like curry powder, mustard and/or Worcester sauce. You could fry an egg or boil some veg and stick those on top. It's really very simple; honest!

■ *Cheese slush*

1 onion	
4/5 tomatoes (fresh or tinned) or	2/3 oz. grated cheese
1/2 tbsp. tomato purée	Worcester sauce
3 cooked potatoes	2 eggs
slice of ham, or 2/3 bacon rashers	marge or other fat
(or bits)	salt and paprika

Preparation and cooking: about 20 mins.
Serves: 2

Melt the fat and fry the chopped onion in it slowly, until it's soft but not brown.
Meanwhile skin and chop the tomatoes (if used) and chop the bacon.
Add these to the onions and cook until warmed through.
Dice the potatoes and add them to the mess with a little water.
Cook the lot for about five minutes.
Meanwhile, boil about $\frac{1}{2}$ pint of water, put it in another pan and crack two eggs into it. Let them simmer until needed.
Just before serving, add the grated cheese, salt and paprika, with a few drops of Worcester sauce.
Serve with the poached egg placed on top.

■ *Macaroni cheese*

12 oz. macaroni	small bay leaf
2 oz. fat	pinch mace
$\frac{3}{4}$ pt. milk	level tsp. salt
dollop of mustard, amount	white pepper
according to strength	1 oz. flour
1 tsp. vinegar	4 oz. grated cheese
slice onion, or more as liked	

Preparation and cooking: about 30 mins.
Serves: 3/4

Boil the milk up with the onion, herbs and seasoning.
Cover it and leave to cool.

Cook the macaroni according to the directions on the packet and test for readiness by spearing a bit with a fork and tasting it. It should taste soft, but *not* mushy.

While the macaroni cooks, make the sauce.

Melt half the fat in a pan, stir in the flour and mustard and leave to cook for a couple of minutes over a *low* heat.

Add the milk through a sieve, if you have one, stirring well all the time.

Boil up slowly, to avoid lumps.

Add the vinegar, remove from the heat and put in all but a sprinkling of cheese. Stir and taste, then add salt, pepper etc., as necessary.

Drain the macaroni.

Melt the rest of the fat, add the macaroni and coat it.

Remove from the heat, put into a heatproof dish and pour the sauce over. Sprinkle the remaining cheese onto it, and cook for about 10 minutes under the grill.

For a change, you could add breadcrumbs to the cheese, or grill some bacon and chuck that in too.

■ *Cheese pudding*

4 oz. grated cheese	2 eggs
4 oz. fresh breadcrumbs (about 4 slices)	cayenne pepper
1 pt. milk	$\frac{1}{2}$ tsp. dry mustard or a little more "wet"
1 oz. marge	salt and pepper

Preparation and cooking: about 1 hour.
Serves: 3/4

Warm the milk, but don't boil it.

Take it off the heat and add the breadcrumbs to soak. Drop in the marge, which should melt.

Turn on the oven (gas 5, 375F, 180C), to let it heat up.

Grease an ovenproof dish – one containing about $1\frac{1}{2}$ pints.

Crack the egg whites into a large bowl, keeping separate from the yolks which you can put in a cup.

Beat the egg whites until they're stiff.

Mix the mustard and cheese together and stir in the yolks.

Add the lot to the soaking breadcrumbs. Stir it all round well, and carefully stir in the whites so that they disperse properly.

Put the dish into the oven, and bake for 40–45 minutes, or until well-browned.

You could put small potatoes into the oven at the same time if you like, and bake the two together. Salad goes well with the pudding, too.

■ *Gloster pie*

cheese sandwiches made with 4 rounds of bread
(preferably stale ones – left-overs from the canteen?)
1 tbsp. tomato purée
1 tomato (optional)
3 fl. oz. milk (about half a mug)
1 small egg
dash of mustard
a knob of marge
salt and pepper
packet/tin of spinach

Preparation and cooking: about 1 hr. 15 mins.
Serves: 2

Chop the crusts off the sandwiches, and spread some tomato purée in the middle. If you use a fresh tomato, slice it and slip that into the sandwich too – thus you have two cheese and tomato sandwiches and the clever bit to come.

Grease an ovenproof dish and, if you're using spinach, spread that over the bottom. Arrange the sandwiches on top, having quartered them.

Whisk together the milk, egg, mustard and salt and pepper, and pour it over the sandwiches.

Leave it to stand until all the liquid has been soaked up – about half-an-hour – then dot the top with marge.

Cook it in the oven on Gas mark 5 (375F or 190C) for about 30 minutes, and then eat.

I didn't like the sound of this when I heard of it – having developed an aversion to cheese sandwiches through over-exposure to them. Surprisingly, it tasted delicious; I'll never look at a stale sandwich in the same way again.

■ *Sweetcorn crumble*

small packet frozen sweet corn (about 8 oz.)
2 oz. breadcrumbs
handful of grated cheese
1 small carton of yoghurt
1 small egg
pinch rosemary (or other herb)
salt and pepper

Preparation and cooking: about 40 mins.
Serves: 2

Boil about half a pint of water, add salt and then sweetcorn.
Boil for 2/3 minutes and drain.

Beat the egg and mix it with everything except the cheese and half the breadcrumbs; mix those two together separately.

Splodge the sweetcorn mixture into a heatproof dish and top it with the cheese and breadcrumbs.

Cook it in the oven at Gas mark 6 (400F or 200C) for about 30 minutes.

Chicken

■ *Casserole for old birds*

2 lb. bird (boiling fowl)   salt and pepper
tin tomatoes   herbs as you like
any other odd veg

Preparation and cooking: about 2 hours.
Serves: 3

Wash the chicken and remove any giblets.
Put it in a big lidded dish.
Chuck the tomatoes over.
Chop the veg and throw them in too.
Cook on a low heat (Gas 2/3, 300F, 150C) for about 2 hours.
(For other weights, calculate the cooking time at 40 minutes per pound).

    There are two main advantages of this recipe: 1) a boiling fowl is much cheaper than a roasting one, and 2) you can make an extra meal by boiling up the giblets and bones later, with a few veg, to make soup.

■ *Chicken and mushroom casserole*

2 chicken legs or thighs   mug (about ½ pt.) hot water
1/2 rashers bacon (or bits)   stock cube
small onion   thyme
2/3 oz. mushrooms

Preparation and cooking: about 1¼ hours.
Serves: 2

Chop the bacon, onion and mushrooms.
Wash the chicken and pat dry.
Chuck everything into a heatproof casserole dish.
Put it in the oven (Gas 4, 350F, 180C), and cover.
Forget it for about an hour.

Eggs

■ *Omelette*

2 eggs
fat for frying
1 tbsp. water or milk
salt and pepper

Preparation and cooking: about 10 mins.
Serves: 1

Heat the fat until it's smoking. Meanwhile, beat the eggs and the water (or milk).
Pour the mixture into the pan and keep it moving, by tilting the pan or using a spatula at the edges.
If the fat's too cool when you add the egg, it won't take: in that case, be more energetic with the spatula and pretend you wanted scrambled eggs anyway.
Before serving, you can add an enormous variety of fillings, such as grated cheese, chopped ham, chopped mushrooms.
Fold the finished article in half (which makes it easier to get out of the pan), and serve.

■ *Quick soufflé*

1 egg
2 tsp. flour (pref. self-raising)
$\frac{1}{2}$ mug milk ($\frac{1}{4}$ pt)

handful of grated cheese
knob of fat
salt

Preparation and cooking: about 10 mins.
Serves: 1

This is really just a superior omelette, but almost easier to make.
Whisk everything together except the fat and cheese.
Heat the fat, pour in the mixture and cook as for omelette or scrambled egg.
Top the cooked egg with grated cheese and brown under the grill if you like.

■ *Eggs in the nest*

1 lb. potatoes
2 egg yolks (optional)
1 oz. fat
2 tbsp. milk (the top, if poss.)
1 tsp. minced onion or herbs
(nutmeg's nice)
4 eggs
salt and pepper

Preparation and cooking: about 40 mins.
Serves: 4

Peel the potatoes (because you're going to mash them in the end)
and cut into small, equal sizes.
Put into boiling, salted water and cook until soft (about 15 mins).
Drain carefully, and mash with a fork and elbow-grease.
Heat the milk, fat, seasoning and herbs.
Take off the heat before the milk's boiled, and add the potato.
Mix it together, and add the egg yolks if you're using them.
Beat well over a low heat.
Put the ready potatoes in an oven-proof dish, leaving space in the
centre.
Boil the eggs in salted water for five mins., shell and add to the dish.
Brown under the grill.
Grated cheese on the top will add flavour to this meal.

■ *Eggs scramble grand-mère*

2 slices bread
2/3 eggs
2 tbsp. milk
salt and pepper

Preparation and cooking: about 10
mins.
Serves: 1/2

You can do scrambled eggs on toast: this is virtually the same. Don't ask me why it's called "grand-mère"; the reader who sent it in didn't explain.

Beat the eggs with the milk, salt and pepper.

Melt the fat in the pan.

Start toasting the bread.

Add the eggs to the pan and cook over a gentle heat.

Stir the eggs in between checking the toast and chopping it into squares when done.

Add the chopped toast just as the egg's ready.

This is tasty served with green salad.

■ *Egg chasseur*

1 small onion
2 oz. mushrooms
oil
2 tbsp. flour
$\frac{1}{2}$ pt. red wine (if you're rich;
otherwise, use stock)
1 tsp. sugar (optional)
1 tsp. mustard
4 tbsp. tomato puree
2 eggs
2 slices of bread

Preparation and cooking: about 15 mins.
Serves: 2

Chop the onion and mushrooms, while you're slowly heating the oil.

Fry them gently in the oil, and add the flour.

Gently add the $\frac{1}{2}$ pint of liquid, stirring all the time to avoid lumps.

Add everything else except the eggs and bread, and simmer.

Meanwhile, toast the bread, boil up some water.

Crack the eggs into the water and let them poach for about 3 mins.

Remove eggs from their pan, put them on the toast and pour the sauce over the lot.

■ *Piperade*

4 slices bread	1 onion	oil/fat
2 eggs	1 green pepper	salt and pepper
2 tomatoes		

Preparation and cooking: about 15 mins.
Serves: 2

Chop the onion and pepper, being careful to get rid of all the pepper's seeds.
Warm the oil and add the veg. Fry them till they're soft.
Add the salt, pepper and any other herbs you fancy.
Beat the eggs lightly and add them to the mixture in the pan.
At the same time, toast the bread.
Fry the pan-mix until the eggs are done, and plonk it all onto the toast.

■ *Eggy macaroni*

6–8 oz. macaroni	3 oz. mushrooms	1 oz. butter
2 cloves garlic	2 oz. marge	salt and pepper
2 eggs		

Preparation and cooking: about 25 mins.
Serves: 2

Boil the eggs for about 5 minutes.
At the same time, boil the macaroni according to the packet directions, until it's soft but not mushy.
Chop the garlic and heat it gently in the melted marge.
Cut the mushrooms into small pieces, and heat them very gently in the butter (actually, you could avoid trouble and pans, by frying the garlic and mushrooms together in less fat).
When done, drain the macaroni and return it to the pan.
Add the mushrooms and garlic (if you've cooked the garlic separately, chuck that away and just use the juice).
Add plenty of salt and pepper, mixing it all gently over a low heat.
Crack the eggs and cut in half, then put them in an oven-proof dish.

Pour the other mixture over and put under the grill or in a warm oven for a few minutes to heat through.

You could add bacon bits to this recipe, if you have them. Fry them up with the mushrooms.

■ *Egg and bacon pasty*

8–10 oz. shortcrust pastry (or flaky)	3–4 eggs
	6–7 oz. bacon bits
1 medium turnip/small swede	2 tbsp. chopped parsley
1 medium potato	pepper

Preparation and cooking: about 1½ hours
Serves: 4

Line a heatproof plate or flan ring with the pastry, using just over half the pastry. Don't let it go much over the edge, unless you want a wodge of pure pastry all round.

Roll out the top to fit and keep it in a cool place.

Chop the bacon up small, after de-fatting it.

Peel the veg if you're going to, chop them into sticks and put them in cold water.

Lightly beat the eggs.

Put half the potato bits on the pastry-lined plate.

Cover with half the bacon bits.

Add half the strips of turnip or swede.

Repeat, but save the potato layer until last. Add parsley.

Damp the pastry lid.

Pour the beaten egg over the pie (*before* adding the lid).

Add the pastry lid and press the edges together. Knock it up with a knife and decorate with a fork, if you're feeling fancy.

Add 1 tablespoon of water to any egg-dregs, and brush it over the top of the pasty.

Put in the oven. Shortcrust pastry needs Gas 5 (375F, 190C) for 25–30 mins: flaky pastry should be on Gas 6 (400F, 200C) for 25–30 mins.

Both shortcrust and flaky pasties should be cooked for a further 25–30 minutes on Gas 3 (325F, 150C).

Fish

■ *Scrambled haddock*

6–8 oz. smoked haddock
2 eggs
2 tbsp. milk
knob marge
2 slices bread
lemon juice/lemon wedges

Preparation and cooking: about 15 mins.
Serves: 2

Bring about ½ pint of water to the boil, pour it into a pan, add the fish and cook for about 5 minutes.
Remove and take off the bones; the skin too if you're fussy, and flake the fish.
Heat the marge, beat the eggs and milk together (without any salt; the fish has enough of its own) and scramble them.
Add the fish, and toast the bread.
Serve with lemon juice and/or wedges.

■ *Fish pie*

8 oz. fish fillet (cod/haddock)
1 potato
little milk
dessertsp. flour
a few peas, if liked
salt, pepper and parsley

Preparation and cooking: About 30 mins.
Serves: 1

Peel and slice the potato, and boil it till soft in water with a pinch of salt.
Meanwhile, cook the fish for about five minutes in a little milk.
With a drop more milk and the flour, make a paste.
Remove the fish from the pan and crumble it into a heat-proof dish.

Add the paste to the fishstock and milk with salt, pepper and parsley. Add the peas too, if you're using them.

Bash the potato with a fork until it's almost mashed.

Pour the milk paste over the fish and spoon the potato round the edge of the dish.

Brown in the oven or under the grill.

■ *Scrapped fish chowder*

8 oz. fish scraps (from
fishmongers)
piece of bacon
small onion
$\frac{1}{2}$ tbsp. flour (optional)
1 potato
$\frac{1}{4}$ pt. milk
pepper
herbs (dill or parsley is tasty)

Preparation and cooking: about 30 mins.
Serves: 1

Boil half a pan of water, slightly salted.

Throw in the fish scraps and boil for about 15 mins. Strain.

Meanwhile, slice the potato and keep in a bowl of water.

Peel and chop the onion, and lightly fry the bacon in its own fat.

When the bacon's done, take it out, drain it and lightly fry the onion in any remaining fat.

Add to the onion the fish stock and sliced potato, pepper and herbs. Cook until the potatoes are tender.

Then add any bits of fish that are left, some milk and cook the lot for about five minutes.

■ *Ciappino*

The ingredients and method are exactly as above, except that tomatoes and extra pepper replace the potato and milk.

Lamb

■ *Breast of lamb*

1 boned breast of lamb
carrots/onions/celery etc. to
make 8 ozs.

Preparation and cooking about $2\frac{1}{4}$ hours.
Serves: 1

Chop the lamb in squares and pack in a pan with the chopped veg on
top, a drop of water and some salt.
Cook in a low oven (Gas 3, 325F, 150C) for about two hours.
You could do baked potatoes in the oven at the same time.
   This meal may not sound much, but it is very cheap for meat, and
tastes fine when you're hungry!

■ *Lamb sweetbreads*

4 oz. packet sweetbreads
(you can buy these frozen from
supermarkets)
2 oz. bacon bits
small onion
1 carrot
2 tbsp. water
1 veg stock cube
wine/cider
salt and pepper

Preparation and cooking: overnight + 1 hour.
Serves: 1

This takes ages, but not too much trouble. It also keeps.
Thaw the sweetbreads, cover with cold water and bring to the boil.
A film of slime might appear; don't worry, just skim it off.
Simmer for 2 minutes, no more. Drain the sweetbreads and put

them on a small plate. Cover that with another, weighted plate and
leave in a cool place over night.
Next day, light fry some bacon in a pan with a sliced onion and some
grated carrot, salt, pepper and any herbs you fancy.
Add the sweetbreads and a glass of wine or cider and vegetable stock
(made with boiling water).
Simmer everything for about 45 minutes with the lid of the pan on,
Serve hot or cold on a slice of toast.

Lasagne

■ *Vegetarian lasagne*

6 oz. lasagne
3 oz. breadcrumbs
3 oz. chopped nuts
8 oz. cottage cheese
Cheese sauce mix (if you're avoiding packets and want a better taste,
use the cheese sauce given in the recipe for *Macaroni cheese*. Double
the quantities of milk, fat and flour)
2 beaten eggs
salt and pepper
clove garlic, crushed

Preparation and cooking: about 1 hour.
Serves: 3

Grease a flattish dish.
Mix all the ingredients, except the lasagne, and the cheese sauce.
Cook the lasagne for 7 mins.
Fill the dish with alternate layers of lasagne and mixture.
Make up the cheese sauce, pour it over the lot and bake for about 40
minutes at Gas 5 (375F, 190C).

This is by far the simplest lasagne brew I've ever seen. If you try
it, like it and feel you're missing the meat, try the following, which
is a bit more difficult.

■ *Meat lasagne*

6 oz. lasagne
tin tomatoes
12 oz. minced meat
1 largish onion
1 tbsp. tomato purée
cheese sauce mix (or the one in the recipe for *Macaroni cheese*, doubled)
salt, pepper
1/2 cloves garlic, crushed
herbs (mixed Italian are good) and a bay leaf

Preparation and cooking: about 1½ hours.
Serves: 3/4

Grease a flattish dish.
Make the meat sauce by cooking the minced meat in its own fat until browned. If you want, drain the minced meat and get rid of some of the juices, before frying the onion and garlic in the remainder. Don't let them brown.
Add the tomato purée and tinned tomatoes, salt, pepper, herbs and bay leaf.
Let is stew while you're making the cheese sauce.
If you like your lasagne soggy, boil the strips in a lot of water for about 5 minutes, until just on the verge of softness. Remove and stretch out individually so that they don't stick. You don't have to do this; but it is a precaution against crunchy pasta.
Put a layer of lasagne at the bottom of the dish, add the meat sauce and cheese sauce. Finish with the cheese sauce, adding some grated cheese if you've any left. Cook in an oven, Gas 4 (350F, 180C) for about 45 minutes.

If you want the lasagne to stand up alone, make sure the cheese sauce is thick, and that you use more meat than juice when layering the meat sauce. I must admit that I've never succeeded with a solid lasagne: I know there's something wrong, but it still tastes pretty good.

Liver

■ *Fried liver*

4 oz. liver (chicken's or lamb's is best)	salt and pepper
	mixed herbs
1 small onion	Worcester sauce/Garam masala
2 oz. bacon bits	fat (pref. oil) for frying
1 tbsp. flour	

Preparation and cooking: about 15 mins.
Serves: 1

Gently heat the oil, while you're chopping the onion and taking the fat off the bacon.

Wash and dry the liver, and dip it in flour (seasoned with the salt, pepper and herbs) so that it's lightly coated).

Gently fry the onion and bacon.

Add the liver and fry quickly, for about 5 minutes on each side at the most.

Add the Worcester sauce or Garam masala at the last minute.

■ *Liver casserole*

8 oz. liver (pref. lamb's)	$\frac{1}{2}$ pt. water with stock cube
1 onion	or 1 small tin of vegetable soup
2/3 oz. bacon bits	8 oz. carrots
2 tbsp. flour	Worcester sauce
salt and pepper	fat (pref. oil) for frying
mixed herbs	

Preparation and cooking: about 1 hour.
Serves: 2

This is an excellent, cheap meal to prove to people that liver is not unpalatable. But, if you don't find lamb's liver and have to use pig's or ox's, soak it in milk for half an hour before use to tenderise it.

Chop the liver into small pieces (about 2 inches round) and dip it in the flour, seasoned with salt, pepper and herbs.

Chop the carrots up very small, and the onion and bacon.

Heat the oil and fry the liver lightly, till it goes brown on the outside.
Put the liver in the bottom of an ovenproof dish.
Lightly fry the onion, carrots and bacon rashers in the remaining fat,
then pile them on top of the liver.
Add the stock or soup, cover the dish and cook it for about 30
minutes in an oven, Gas 3 (325F, 160C).

Macaroni

■ *Macaroni special*

2/3 oz. macaroni (pref. wholemeal)
small pot of cottage cheese
4 oz. veg: mushrooms, courgettes etc.
$\frac{1}{4}$ pt. milk

Preparation and cooking: about 15 mins.
Serves: 1

Put the macaroni with salt into boiling water, and cook for about 10
minutes.
Meanwhile, warm the milk with the vegetables.
Remove the milk from the heat and add the cottage cheese.
When the macaroni is ready, drain it and stir the whole mess
together.

Mince

■ *Shepherd's pie* (basic)

4 oz. minced meat (or cold
leftovers)
1 medium potato (or leftover)
grated cheese, a handful
salt and pepper
herbs as you like

Preparation and cooking: about 45 mins.
Serves: 1

If you're using mince, fry it gently in its own fat, while peeling the potato, chopping it up small and boiling it in salted water until soft. Transfer the meat to an ovenproof dish. Smash the cooked potato with a fork and spread it on top. Season with salt, pepper and herbs. Add the grated cheese.

Either brown under the grill, or put in the oven (Gas 5, 350F, 190C) for about 30 minutes.

■ *Shepherd's pie* ("sophisticated")

1 medium onion
1 small tin tomatoes/2 tbsp.
tomato purée
8 oz. minced meat
2 medium potatoes
1 stock cube
bay leaf
salt and pepper
herbs
grated cheese (optional; parmesan is fine)

Preparation and cooking: about 1 hour.
Serves: 2

Crumble the stock cube into the mince and lightly fry it in its own fat.

Peel and chop the potatoes small, put into boiling water with a pinch of salt and boil till soft.

Remove and drain the mince, saving the juice to fry the onion in.

Fry onions gently, and add the tomatoes, and seasoning.

Add the meat to the onions and keep warm while bashing the potato with a fork.

Put the meat in an ovenproof dish with the potato layer on top.

Add grated cheese if you have any and brown under the grill or put in the oven for about 30 minutes on Gas 5 (350F, 190C).

■ *Cheesy meatballs*

4 oz. minced meat
1 small onion
handful grated cheese

herbs as you fancy them
salt and pepper

Preparation and cooking: about 15–20 mins.
Serves: 1

Grate the onion or chop it finely and mix it with the meat and
seasoning. Add the grated cheese gradually, until there's just
enough to bind everything together.

Out of this concoction make a few small balls, shove them on a
skewer and grill gently for 10–15 minutes. Use the skewer to turn
the meatballs and brown them all over.

■ *Meat loaf*

8 oz. minced meat
1 large onion
1 clove garlic (or a pinch of minced garlic)
1 tbsp. parsley (or a pinch of some other herb)
1 large slice bread
1 tbsp. tomato purée
1 dessertsp. soya sauce
splash of Worcester sauce
1 small egg
salt and pepper

Preparation and cooking: about 2 hrs.
Serves: 2/3

Don't be put off by the time this takes – most of it is oven-time.

Take the crusts off the bread and soak it in the combined purée, soya
and Worcester sauce.

Leave it there while you finely chop the onion and garlic.

Now the messy bit: squeeze the bread in your hands to get rid of
excess moisture, then mix it with the meat, onion, garlic, salt and
pepper.

Beat the egg and add it to the rest. This should bind it. If you need more binding before the loaf will stay put in shape, add a drop or two of oil.

Make a loaf shape, wrap it in foil and cook on Gas mark 4 (350F or 180C) for about 1½ hours. Uncover the top of the loaf for the last 20 minutes or so to brown it.

By the way, this meal tastes fine cold, too.

Mushrooms

■ *Mushroom and nut pilaff*

4 tbsp. flour	2 sticks celery
oil for frying (2 doses)	1 red pepper (or green if
6 oz. rice (fluid)	preferred)
12 fl. oz water	4 oz. (1 cup) cashew nuts
1 large onion	6 oz. mushrooms
1 clove garlic	salt and pepper

Preparation and cooking: about 1 hr. 10 mins.
Serves: 2/3

Before we go anywhere else, remember that rice should always be cooked in twice the amount of water. You should be okay with this if you use one mug of rice and two of water.

Prepare the veg by slicing the onion, chopping the garlic finely, chopping the celery, nuts and mushrooms, and de-seeding and chopping the pepper.

Heat the oil and fry the rice in it for 2/3 minutes, stirring to coat it. Add the boiling water, stir once and cover the pan. Simmer for 40–45 minutes, until the water has disappeared (this might not take so long if you use white rice).

Meanwhile, heat the rest of the oil in a pan and fry the onion gently. Add the other veg and cook slowly for about five minutes. Add the rice, when cooked, and the seasoning, simmering very gently. Stir occasionally and heat the stuff right through.

This is best served with a green salad.

Pizza

■ *Quick pizza*

1 slice bread
tomato purée
pinch of marjoram/other herbs
handful of grated cheese
few mushrooms (optional)

Preparation and cooking: about 5 mins.
Serves: 1

Spread the bread with tomato purée, and sprinkle with herbs, then cheese, and dot any mushrooms around. Grill.

This is a big cheat, really; but good for lazy louts, or non-cookers. If you're more ambitious, try the following:

■ *Pizza from scratch*

1 cup flour
1 tsp. baking powder
salt and pepper
3 tbsp. water
pizza topping: cheese, tomato, salami, anchovy; you can also add: olives, onions, mushrooms, bacon etc.

Preparation and cooking: about 20 mins.
Serves: 1/2

This is a quick pizza, without the yeast, which basically means that it takes less time than other kinds.
Make the dough by mixing the flour, baking powder and salt, and add the water. Knead it with your hands into a smooth dough.
Roll it out into a thick circle – you can use a milk bottle if you're lacking a rolling pin – which fits a small frying pan.
Heat the oil in a frying pan until it's hot, but before it starts smoking. Put in the dough and fry it for five minutes. Turn over, using a spatula. Lay the topping on it and cook for another five minutes.

Pork

■ *Pork casserole*

4 oz. belly pork
1 onion
1 tbsp. tomato purée
1 dessertsp. honey
a pinch (or more) dry mustard

1 sma
½ pint v
salt and ⌐
herbs (ros

Preparation and cooking: about 3–4 hours or 45 mi
Serves: 1

Mix the honey, mustard and seasoning with ½ pint of water.
Put the pork, chopped onion, tomato and a drop more water into an oven-proof dish. Cover it with the honey mixture and put into a slow oven (Gas 3, 325F, 150C) for 3–4 hours. Make sure the pan's covered.
Just before serving, heat the baked beans, add them to the casserole and eat.
If you cook the casserole on the stove, chuck everything except the beans into a pan with 1 pint of water – which should boil away. Cover the simmer for about ¾ hour. Add the baked beans before serving to heat through.

Porridge

Fruity porridge

1 cup liquid (water, milk and water, or milk)
½ cup porridge oats/soya flour

nuts, raisins etc.
banana

Preparation and cooking: about 10 mins.
Serves: 1

This can be eaten for breakfast or, would you believe, as a pudding. Put the liquid, porridge and nuts, raisins into a pan and cook quite gently for about seven minutes. Add a mashed banana, if liked, at the end.

...g water
...ough oats
...ied fruit

Preparation and cooking: about 20 mins.
Serves: 1

This sounds a little less exciting than the previous recipe, but look how it's made (probably while you're getting washed in the morning).
Put the oats and dried fruit into a liddable butter dish or something similar. Add the water and cover for twenty minutes with the lid. Wrap newspaper round the dish to keep in all the heat.

Potato

■ *Potato pancakes*

4 oz. potato (when peeled)
1 egg
1 oz. flour
2/3 fl. oz. milk
fat to fry
2/3 oz. grated cheese
or chopped bacon

Preparation and cooking: about 30 mins.
Serves: 1/2

Grate the potato.
Add seasoning, egg, flour and enough milk to make a thick paste, and let it all stand for about 15 minutes.
Mix in the cheese or (ready-grilled) bacon.
Heat the fat.
Drop spoonfuls of the mixture in, heat until golden brown and then turn them over to cook on the other side.

Rabbit

■ *Wild rabbit*

rabbit joints (1 per person)
veg of any sort
$\frac{1}{2}$ pt. water per person
$\frac{1}{2}$–1 stock cube per person

Preparation and cooking: about 45 mins.
Serves: as you like

Wash the rabbit joints, cover with the herbs you fancy, and chuck into a pan with scraped veg and stock to cover.
Cook on a low heat until soft, covered (about forty minutes per pound).
  You can achieve a crunchy-ish outside effect, by dipping the joints in seasoned flour first and frying them till brown before boiling them up.

Rice

■ *Long grain rice original*

1 cup water: $\frac{1}{2}$ cup rice
salt

Preparation and cooking: see below.
Serves: as you like

The ordinary way to cook rice is by putting it in the pan with salt and boiling water – twice as much water as rice – putting on the lid (after stirring once) and cooking until soft without lifting the lid. Brown rice takes about 30 mins, white rice about half the time. Drain by tipping cold water over to remove starch, and boiling water to re-heat it.
  However, there's a simple way too. By putting the rice and boiling salted water into a vacuum flask, lidding it and leaving for $1\frac{1}{2}$ hours, the rice cooks itself.

■ *Brown rice mash*

2/3 oz. brown rice
tuna, sardines or fried veg

Preparation and cooking: about 35 mins.
Serves: 1

Cook the rice for about 30 minutes, according to directions above.
Towards the end of cooking, add the other bits and heat through.

■ *Brown rice hash* (cold)

brown rice leftovers
hard-boiled eggs
nuts and raisins

Preparation and cooking: about 10 mins.
Serves: 1

Having cooked extra rice the day before (as is the common
"mistake") boil an egg for about 10 minutes until hard, chop it up
and add to the rice with nuts, raisins and whatever else you like.

■ *Risotto*

1 small cup rice   oil for frying
2 small cups water   veg of any sort
salt   mixed herbs
onion   1 tbsp. tomato purée

Preparation and cooking: about 30–45 mins.
Serves: 1

Boil the rice as in the basic recipe.
Meanwhile, gently fry any veg you have in a pan with salt, herbs
and tomato purée.
When the rice is strained, add the veg and heat through.

Rissoles

■ *Monosodium rissoles*

2 tbsp. oil for frying $\frac{1}{2}$ lemon, rind and juice
1 packet of stuffing mix   1 egg

Preparation and cooking: about 15 mins.
Serves: 1

This recipe is strictly against my principles of feeding yourself
healthily, but if you're not bothered or are too knackered to cook
properly, it's easy and tasty.
Mix everything together while the oil is heating in a pan.
Make into rissoles and fry on both sides.

Salads

■ *Coleslaw*

carrots   cauliflower
white cabbage   peppers – or any/all plus others
celery

Preparation: about 15 mins.
Serves: as you like

Grate them all, or chop them small and add a dressing of your own
choice, or one included at the end of the *salads* section.

■ *Red cabbage salad*

red cabbage   nuts and raisins if liked
apple   lemon juice
onion

Preparation: about 15 mins.
Serves: as you like

Peel the onion, and chop that and the apple.
Grate the red cabbage.
Add nuts and raisins.
Mix everything together and sprinkle with lemon juice. You can substitute raw, grated beetroot for the cabbage if you prefer.

■ *Winter salad*

1 carrot	1 leek or any other crunchy veg
½ turnip	yoghurt/salad cream
1 apple	sunflower seeds, nuts etc.

Preparation: about 10 mins.
Serves: 1/2

Chop everything finely and mix with the yoghurt or salad cream. It's almost a meal when you use the nuts; a side-salad if not.

■ *Potato, cress and mushroom salad*

4 – 8 oz. potato, scrubbed
1 box mustard and cress
2 – 4 oz. chopped mushrooms
yoghurt/mayonnaise/oil

Preparation and cooking: about 40 mins.
Serves: 1/2

Cook the scrubbed, chopped potatoes until soft.
Add them to the cress, mushrooms and mix with the dressing (which of course, you've already made up to your taste).

■ *Left-over salad*

cold potato	salad cream *or*
cold meat	oil
raw onion	vinegar
raw carrot	salt and pepper
left-over beans, peas etc.,	

Preparation and cooking: about 10 mins.
Serves: as you like

You can actually use any left-overs for this.
Chop everything small, the onion and carrot smaller than the rest.
If you're using salad cream, mix it in with the salt and pepper.
If you're using oil, vinegar and maybe herbs, try the following:

■ *Salad dressing*

1 part vinegar	salt and pepper
2 parts oil	mixed herbs

Preparation: about 5 mins.
Serves: as you like

Mix together everything and beat very well.
You can add mustard, too, or replace the oil and vinegar with 1 part
lemon juice and 2 parts yoghurt.

Sausagemeat

■ *Sausage sizzles*

8 oz. sausagemeat	herbs
1 egg (optional)	2 tbsp. flour
salt and pepper	oil

Preparation and cooking: about 15 mins.
Serves: 1/2

Mix together sausagemeat, herbs, salt and pepper, and a beaten egg
if you're using it.
Coat with flour while the oil is heating, having formed into
rissole-shapes.
Fry on both sides.
These taste much the same as expensive, skinless sausages and are
much cheaper!

■ *Sausagemeat and pasta*

8 oz. sausages	1 clove garlic
2/3 oz. pasta	mixed herbs
1 large/2 medium onions	pinch of chilli powder
1 red/green pepper	knob of fat
1 small tin tomatoes	salt and pepper

Preparation and cooking: about 45 mins.
Serves: 2

Fry the onions and pepper gently in the fat for about 5 minutes.
Meanwhile, boil the water for the pasta.
Add tomatoes to the onion, plus all the other flavourings.
Let them simmer while you're grilling the sausage.
Boil and drain the pasta.
Mix together the pasta, veg and about 1 pint of water.
When the sausages are ready, add to the rest and simmer for 10 to 15 minutes.
This meal is tasty with bread and pickles.

Spaghetti

■ *Spaghetti leftovers*

2/3 oz. spaghetti
peas
tuna
garlic salt
salt

Preparation and cooking: about 15 mins.
Serves: 1

Boil the spaghetti in lots of salted water until it's just soft enough to eat, keeping the pan lid on while it's cooking.
Drain the spaghetti and add the rest.

■ *Quick spaghetti*

2/3 oz. spaghetti
1 small tin tomatoes or some
tomato juice
1 oz. breadcrumbs
or (still using the spaghetti and
tomatoes)

1 tbsp. oatmeal
2 tbsp. soya mince (cooked for
five mins)

Preparation and cooking: about 20 mins.
Serves: 1

Boil the spaghetti in lots of salted water, until soft.
Meanwhile, heat the tomatoes and re-constituted soya, if used.
Drain the spaghetti and pile anything else on.
Vegans can eat this as it is; vegetarians and others might like to top
with grated cheese.
   It's tasty with salad.

Useful recipe books

If you're not satisfied with the preceding recipes, or would like to
try others (including puddings), get hold of some of the following
books. Top of the stakes with people I've talked to is *Cooking in a
bedsitter* (details below), but all those listed are worth looking at.
Most are paperback and cheap if you can't find them in the library.

Cooking in a bedsitter, Katherine Whitehorn (Penguin)
Food for one, Deanna Brostoff (available from Sainsbury's branches)
Easy cooking for one or two and *More easy cooking for one or two*, Louise
   Davies (Penguin): both are meant for the elderly, but there are
   some interesting and, for us, curious, recipes in them.
The first time cook book, Evelyn and Judi Rose (Penguin)
The pauper's cookbook, Jocasta Innes (Penguin)
Frugal food, Delia Smith (Coronet)
How to cheat at cooking, Delia Smith (Coronet)
Vegetarian kitchen, Sarah Brown (BBC Publications)
The complete vegetarian cookbook, Janet Hunt (Hamlyn)

The colour book of wholefood cookery, Carole Hardslip (Octopus Books)
Bean feast, Rose Elliott (White Eagle Publishing Trust)
The bean book, Rose Elliott (Fontana)
Not just a load of old lentils, Rose Elliott (Fontana)
Simply delicious, Rose Elliot (Fontana)
Recipes for a small planet, Ellen Buchanan Ewald (Ballantine)
Country fare, Sheila Howarth (Granada)
Raw energy, Leslie and Susannah Kenton (Century)

Additionally, supermarket chains such as Tesco and Sainsbury sell interesting cooking leaflets and books. Delve in there.

For vegetarians, information and ideas can be obtained from *The British Vegetarian Society*, 53 Marloes Rd, London W8 6LA (01 937 7739).

Vegans should write to: *The Vegans Society*, 47, Highlands Road, Leatherhead, Surrey.

And if you're worried that you might be allergic to certain foods, it's worth reading *Not all in the mind* by Dr. Richard Mackerness, (Pan).

6. Miscellaneous odds and sods

London life ■ useful addresses ■ useful books

London life

The best place to visit first when you arrive as a fresher new to London is a bookstall, where you'll find the *Time Out London Student Guide*. It's newly issued every year; it's concise, and it contains almost everything you want to know about London life.

Student life in any big city can come as a shock, especially if you're from "rural parts". You're very lucky in that there is a lot of cheap or even free entertainment around: public art galleries and museums, parks and enormous department stores all cost nothing (initially) and are fascinating to wander around. London has the added bonus of "spontaneous" happenings in underground subways, market places and Covent Garden. In fact, if you can brave the crowds, any busy street can be entertaining.

Since most large cities have a high student population, student facilities and special offers abound – your problem is to find out about them!

Accommodation

Worse than in the country generally is the accommodation situation. Rents in London easily take care of the extra grant you receive – unless you're lucky or squatting – and places are hard to find.

Rather than search only in the immediate college environs, look around the cheaper residential areas (after sussing out the transport situation): Acton, Camden, the East End and South-east London are just a few of the likely spots. You might find that sharing a house, when you know others in the same boat, is the cheapest way to live.

If you're stuck without a home when you arrive in the city, see the college's accommodation officer. As well as giving you useful addresses for semi-permanent homes, he/she might be able to put you in touch with hostels where you can stay while you're house/flat-hunting. Some of these places are pretty squalid, some are pricey, but they're providing you with a roof – and probably a strong incentive to find somewhere quick!

The Students' Union, at college, if not the accommodation officer, will direct you towards organisations specially catering for your needs. There are a few addresses which might be worth visiting at the end of this guide, too.

Transport

When you do eventually find somewhere to live, make sure that college is easily accessible from there. As I've said before: after Shanks's pony, a bike is the cheapest form of travel – but very nickable. Take the precautions suggested in Chapter 1, *Travel* section.

Although London isn't the den of crime and iniquity that the uninitiated might believe, it does contain a hell of a lot of people, and some of them are thieves. Underground stations are notorious haunts for pickpockets and other hasslers, so don't be easy prey.

Always look as if you know where you're going, even if you haven't really the foggiest idea: be armed with an underground map to prevent having to search for one in the station (which isn't always easy) – main stations give them away.

Any bag you carry should, obviously, be closed. If possible, keep your fare in a handy pocket – the same with your ticket. When you do stop, keep any bag you're carrying between your feet. Leaving it unattended asks for either of two problems: it might be nicked, or it might be carted off by rail staff/police who'll think it's an unexploded bomb.

If you're worried about being mugged, don't get hysterical; the proportion of travellers who encounter hassles is still very low. But do take precautions: carry a pepper pot to throw at any "nasty" if you like, or some lemon juice. There are also plenty of self-defence classes around. Remember that you're only likely to discover how sensible it is to be on the alert if you're caught unawares.

Incidentally, people tend to become more off-guard during hot weather: don't do that; thieves are aware of that relaxed attitude too.

Entertainment

The best guides to cheap (or expensive) entertainment in London are *Time Out* and *City Limits*, both weekly magazines.

But remember, wherever you go, to take your NUS card with you. Many exhibitions offer cheap entry to students; many theatres have student reductions, too. Some theatres insist that their student tickets are sold only on the day of performance, so watch for that. For ardent theatre-goers who like quality seats, visit the booth in Leicester Square. On performance day it sells theatre tickets off at half-price or thereabouts; but this service is for anyone with no extra student concessions. It also tends to offer only the more pricey seats.

Generally, the biggest hazard for the city student is over-spending, because there's always something interesting around at a price. Try to stick to the cheaper pastimes and have fun that way. It's untrue to say that London or any city is unfriendly, and you don't have to pay to make friends. If you're lost, find a place you like the look of and visit it regularly; and don't be shy to talk to strangers (but do be wary of accepting their offers!). See the list on the next few pages to discover possibilities of getting into "your thing".

Useful addresses

If you write to any of the following, don't expect a reply unless you enclose a stamped addressed envelope.

London

■ *London generally*
London Students' Union, University of London Union, Malet Street, London WC1. Tel. 01 637 5892 (there is a nursery for the kids of students and college staff)

International Students' House, 229, Great Portland Street, London W1. Tel. 01 631 3223 (this runs a social club)

London Tourist Board, 26, Grosvenor Gardens, London SW1. Tel. 01 730 3488

■ *Accommodation*

Housing Advice Switchboard, 47, Charing Cross Road, London WC2. Tel. 01 434 2522

London Youth Advisory Centre, 26, Prince of Wales Road, NW5. Tel. 01 269 4792/3

■ *Help!* (personal)

Capital Helpline, Tel. 01 388 7575 (for emotional problems)

Gay Icebreakers (Men), Tel: 01 274 9590

Gay Switchboard, Tel. 01 837 7324

London Friend (for gays), 274, Upper Street, Islington, London N1.

London Gay Teenage Group, Tel. 01 274 5741

Lesbian Line, Tel. 01 251 6911

Greater London Association for Disabled People, (GLAD) 1, Thorpe Close, London W10. Tel. 01 960 5799 (their telephone service offers details of local help)

City Lit Centre for the Deaf, Keeley Street, London WC2. Tel. 01 242 9872 (this centre offers academic advice for deaf ILEA students)

London Rape Crisis Centre, PO Box 69, London WC1. Tel. 01 837 1600 (the telephone is answered 24 hours daily)

London Women's Aid, 52–54, Featherstone Street, London EC1. Tel. 01 251 6537 (this offers legal aid and accommodation to harrassed women)

■ *Legal help*

Mary Ward Legal Centre, 42, Queen Square, London WC1. Tel. 01 831 7000/7009 (non-profit making)

■ *Jobs*

Childminders, 67, Marylebone High Street, London W1. Tel. 01 937 9763 (want to be a baby-sitter?)

Jobs Unlimited, Tel. 01 359 3070

■ *Travel*
Lift Exchange Centre, 14, Broadway, London SW1. Tel. 01 834 9225. (cheap and easy "hitching" service for people who are willing to share petrol costs; there's a small membership fee)
National Express, Victoria Coach Station, Buckingham Palace Road, London SW1. Tel. 01 730 0202. (Bookings: Tel. 01 730 3499)
London Transport Enquiries, Tel. 01 222 1234

■ *British Rail*
British Rail, Fenchurch Street, Liverpool Street Tel. 01 283 7171 (to East Anglia and Essex)
Kings Cross, Tel. 01 278 2477 (to east of England and Scotland)
Broad Street, Euston, St. Pancras, Marylebone. Tel. 01 387 7070 (to Midlands, Northern England, Scotland and North Wales)
Paddington, Tel. 01 262 6767 (to southern Midlands, South-west England and South Wales)
Waterloo, London Bridge, Victoria, Cannon Street, Charing Cross, Holborn and Blackfriars, Tel. 01 928 5100 (to Kent, Surrey, Sussex and Hampshire)

National

■ *Accommodation*
Citizens' Advice Bureaux (look under "C" in the phone book)
Advisory Service for Squatters, 2, St. Paul's Road, London N1. Tel. 01 359 8814 (visits by appointment only)

■ *Insurance*
Endsleigh Insurance Services Ltd, 97, Southampton Row, London WC1. Tel. 01 580 4311
Harrison Beaumont Ltd, 69, High Street, Witney, Oxford. Tel. 0093 3251

■ *Grants and benefits*
National Union of Students, Research Policy Department, NUS, 461 Holloway Road, London N7 6LZ.

■ *Help!* (personal)
Family Planning Association, 27–35, Mortimer Street, London
W1N 7RJ. Tel. 01 636 7866
Gingerbread, 35, Wellington Street, London WC2. Tel. 01 240
0983 (advice for single parents)
National Council for One Parent Families, 255, Kentish Town
Road, London NW5. Tel. 01 267 1361
British Pregnancy Advisory Service, 58, Petty France, London
SW1. Tel. 01 222 0895
Samaritans (under "S" in the phone book)
National Association for Mental Health, (MIND), 22, Harley
Street, London W1. Tel. 01 637 0741

■ *Racial difficulties*
Commission for Racial Equality, Elliot House, 10–12, Allington
Street, London SW1. Tel. 01 828 7022
Joint Council for the Welfare of Immigrants, 115, Old Street,
London EC1. Tel. 01 405 5527 (confidential and legal advice)
United Kingdom Council for Overseas Students' Affairs,
(UKCOSA), 60, Westbourne Grove, London W2. Tel. 01 229
9268/9 (visits by appointment only)
World University Service, 30, Compton Terrace, London N1.
Tel. 01 226 6767 (for refugee students)

■ *Gays*
Gay Switchboard, Tel. 01 237 7324
Campaign for Homosexual Equality, (CHE), BM/CHE, London
WC1N 3XX.
Gay Youth Movement, BM/GYM, London WC1N 3XX.

■ *Disabled*
The Disability Alliance, (Education and Resources Association),
25, Denmark Street, London WC2H 8NJ. Tel. 01 240 0806
(specialises in welfare rights)
National Bureau for Handicapped Students, (NBHS), 40,
Brunswick Square, London WC1N 1AZ. Tel. 01 278 3459
(advice for all disabled students and their helpers)

Royal National Institute for the Blind, (RNIB), 224, Great Portland Street, London W1. Tel. 01 388 1266 (offers student advisors and info on how to get extra grants)

■ *Legal help*
Consumers' Association, 14, Buckingham Street, London WC2. Tel. 01 839 1222
Gay Legal Advice, (GLAD), Tel. 01 821 7672
Law Centres Federation, 164, North Gower Street, London NW1. Tel. 01 387 8570 (or under "L" in the phone book)
National Council for Civil Liberties, (NCCL), 21, Tabard Street, London SE1
Release, 1, Elgin Avenue, London W9. Tel. 01 289 1123 (best known for its advice on drugs and problems with the police)
Welfare Rights, Tel. 01 405 5942/4517

Useful books

■ *The Student Book* (Published each year by Macmillan)
■ *It's never too late . . .* a practical guide to continuing education for women of all ages, by Joan Perkin (published by Impact Books)
■ *Know your rights* (published by the National Council for Civil Liberties, 21 Tabard Street, London SE1 4LA)
■ *First Rights – a Guide to Legal Rights for Young People* (also published by the NCCL)
■ *Well-being: helping yourself to good health* by Robert Eagle (published by Penguin Books)
■ *Make it Happy* by Jane Cousins (published by Penguin Books)
■ *Hitchhikers Manual: Britain* and *Europe: a Manual for Hitchhikers* both by Simon Calder (published by Vacation Work Publications, 9 Park End Street, Oxford OX1 1HJ)
■ *The Hitchhiker's Guide to Europe* by Ken Welsh (published by Pan Books)
■ *Working Holidays* (published by the Central Bureau for Educational Visits and Exchanges, Seymour Mews House, London W1H 9PE)

Help Yourself
An everyday survival handbook
Alastair Thomson and Rosemary Platt

Help Yourself is a practical guide to everyday living aimed
particularly at young people. In an easily readable and lively style it
provides hard factual information as well as tips and useful advice
about:
  getting a job
  coping with money
  finding accommodation
  claiming benefits
  looking after your health
  getting involved in the community
  knowing your rights

Help Yourself gets behind the jargon of rules, regulations and red
tape to give the facts clearly, together with suggestions on how to
find out more and make the most of all opportunities available.

ISBN 0 245-54281-7   £2.95

impact books are distributed by Harrap Ltd, 19–23 Ludgate Hill,
London EC4M 7PD (Tel. 01 248 6444)